HOME DECORATING
with
Fabric

HOME DECORATING

with Fabric

MORE THAN 80 GREAT PROJECTS FROM CUSHIONS TO COMFORTERS

Carol Parks

Sterling Publishing Co., Inc. New York
A Sterling/Lark Book

Editor: **DAWN CUSICK**
Art Director: **CHRIS BRYANT**
Production: **ELAINE THOMPSON, CHRIS BRYANT**
Proofreading: **JULIE BROWN**
Illustrations: **KAY HOLMES STAFFORD**

Library of Congress Cataloging-in-Publication Data

Parks, Carol, 1942-
    Home decorating with fabric : more than 80 great projects from cushions to
comforters / by Carol Parks.
      p.   cm.
    "A Sterling/Lark book."
    Includes index.
    ISBN 0-8069-3158-2
    1. Household linens.   2. Home furnishings.   3. Textile fabrics in interior
decoration.   4. Machine sewing. I. Title.
TT387.P37   1995
646.2'1—dc20   95-4590
                                                CIP

10 9 8 7 6 5 4 3 2 1

A Sterling/Lark Book

Published by Sterling Publishing Co., Inc.
387 Park Avenue South, New York, NY 10016

Created and produced by Altamont Press, Inc.
50 College Street, Asheville, NC 28801

© 1995, Altamont Press

English translation © 1995, Altamont Press

All photos © Ariadne/Spaarnestad, Utrecht, Holland.

Distributed in Canada by Sterling Publishing,
    c/o Canadian Manda Group, One Atlantic Ave., Suite 105,Toronto, Canada M6K 3E7
Distributed in Great Britain and Europe by Cassell PLC
    Wellington House, 125 Strand, London WC2R 0BB, England
Distributed in Australia by Capricorn Link (Australia) Pty Ltd.,P.O. Box 6651, Baulkam Hills, Business Centre,
    NSW 2153,Australia

Printed in Hong Kong

ISBN 0-8069-3158-2

Introduction

It's wonderful to see that the current trend in home decorating is toward individual expression. Eclectic furnishings, off-beat color schemes, and anachronistic combinations appear regularly in decorating magazine features. "Home" has become a showcase for its occupants' ideas, tastes, talents, and preferences, the elements combined in a manner that exactly suits its residents' lifestyle.

Creative use of fabrics plays an important role in every decorating scheme. A length of material can make a substantial change in the feel of a room, yet requires a relatively small expenditure of money and time. Redecorating with fabrics is a great deal more fun than the tedious and messy job of scraping and repainting, and it's far less costly than investing in new furniture.

Even a small amount of fabric yardage can make an important difference. Pillow covers in bright colors will warm a winter-dreary room, then can be replaced with cool colors for visual relief from summer's heat. Fabric allows for quick, temporary change, too: festive place mats and napkins add to holiday parties; cheery covers dress up the folding chairs pressed into service for large family gatherings.

Fabrics can serve to unify the elements of a room. Cushions of the same fabric for six different dining chairs creates a room that says "creatively decorated" rather than "assembled from cast-offs." Drapery and upholstery fabric scraps are the starting point for hundreds of small decorating projects.

Decorating with fabric has practical advantages too. Fabric will deaden sound and insulate against cold or heat. Durable, washable fabric offers protection—as in a slipcover for a silk-upholstered antique chair—just until the children grow up.

Decorating projects provide inveterate fabric collectors a multitude of ways to justify their accumulations. Pieces of heirloom needlework, bargain remnants, and even recylcled fabric treasures convert readily to interesting—and personalized—elements in a decorating scheme.

There are projects here for beginning sewers as well as for those with experience—and several require no sewing at all. Complete instructions are included for all the projects shown in the photographs. In addition, there are instructions for dozens of sewing techniques that can be incorprated in your own original designs. Some projects, such as slipcovers, involve careful planning and relatively large quantities of fabric. Others are just for fun and can be completed easily in a single Sunday afternoon.

We hope you'll find this collection useful and inspiring for the projects it includes, but better yet, that it will serve to inspire your own ideas for decorating with fabric.

Tools *and* Equipment

Every book to do with sewing contains a list of essential equipment, the tools that belong in every sewing room and which any person reading a sewing book no doubt has on hand: a sewing machine, a good steam iron, a flexible tape measure, sharp shears kept just for cutting fabric, and a collection of hand sewing needles. Then there is another list, the tools and gadgets considered essential by one sewer and never used by the next. My own list of essentials follows, along with the reasons I can't do without them. Many of these items particularly are helpful for certain kinds of projects and are mentioned in the instructions for those specific projects.

WORKSPACE

An organized and well-equipped work space will make any project go more smoothly. For decorating projects that require working with large pieces of fabric, it is especially important to have enough space to work. A good-sized table is essential for laying out and straightening fabric and for accurate cutting and pinning. It's helpful, too, to be able to leave everything in place between sewing sessions. Perhaps the dining room can be "borrowed" from the family while the project is in progress. Another option is to rent a long folding table for the duration.

SEWING MACHINE

Any machine, regardless of its vintage or level of sophistication, will work best if it receives regular attention. A minor problem, such as stitch tension that's slightly out of adjustment, can be a major headache with a project like a slipcover that involves miles of seams.

Before beginning each sewing project, clean the machine thoroughly to remove all the lint from the bobbin area, the top of the needle bar, and under the feed dogs. If the model requires oiling, follow the instructions in the owner's manual.

It is essential to replace the needle on a regular basis. This simple act is an inexpensive cure for a great percentage of all sewing machine ills. The needle has a limited life expectancy, and once past its prime can aggravate in a number of ways: skipped stitches, puckered seams, pulled threads, or holes in the fabric to name a few. Tough fabrics such as tightly woven synthetics and heavily finished home decorating fabrics will dull a needle quickly. Hitting a pin calls for immediate replacement, since a bent needle can in turn damage the bobbin hook, a real calamity.

Use the needle type recommended in the owner's manual. The size and point style should be appropriate for the fabric being sewn. Needle manufacturers have doubled their offerings over the past few years to accommodate changes in fabrics, threads, and machine technology. There are special needles for sewing tough fabrics, fragile fabrics, and knits, as well as for stitching with metallic threads or heavy rayon threads. There are others designed just for machine embroidery and decorative stitching. Check with a dealer who sells accessories for your machine to see what's new. And if a particular fabric or project is causing difficulties, take a sample to the dealer. It may be there is a specialized needle to solve the problem.

SERGER

The overlock machine's forte is its ability to stitch a seam, trim it, and overcast the raw edges in a single step. A serger can reduce by hours the time required to make draperies, slipcovers, or other projects that involve sewing miles of plain seams. A major decorating project provides a good excuse for investing in a serger.

The serger needs the same attention as a sewing machine. It should be cleaned and oiled even more frequently because of the prodigious amounts of lint it produces. It too requires a regular change of needles. The upper knife blade needs to be checked regularly as well to make sure it is sharp and free of nicks.

SCISSORS AND SHEARS

In addition to basic shears, small trimming scissors with thick blades are very handy. And pinking shears are a good alternative to overcasting seams on lighter weight fabrics.

ROTARY CUTTER AND MAT

These tools save hours of cutting time. They are indispensable for making perfectly straight cuts, particularly on the bias, and for cutting through multiple layers of fabric.

STRAIGHT PINS

Best for general use are fairly long, slender glass-headed "silk" pins. They are easy to see in the fabric, and won't melt if touched with a hot iron. The longer and heavier quilters' pins are useful for large projects and thick fabrics.

CARPENTER'S SQUARE

Made of heavy metal, it's excellent to use with rotary cutter for perfect square corners.

TUBE TURNERS

Most useful is a set of sturdy brass tubes in various sizes, with spiral-tipped wires for drawing the tube through.

BIAS TAPE MAKERS

These metal gadgets instantly shape bias fabric strips into double-fold tape. They are available in several sizes to make tape of different widths.

EXPANDING METAL GAUGE

This adjustable gauge will divide a given area into evenly spaced increments. It's a great timesaver for marking placement of buttons, buttonholes, drapery pleats, and the like.

CORNER TEMPLATE

Here's help in achieving perfect and equal corners on pillows, chair covers, etc. The metal device offers a choice of four corner styles and holds the fabric in place for pressing.

MARKING TOOLS

There is a staggering number of fabric markers available. Every single one of them should be tested on a scrap when it's to be used on a new piece of fabric. Even the safest marking pen ink can react unpredictably with the dye or finishing agent in a fabric. Favorites are the water soluble marking pen and fine-line chalk marker—the kind with the metal wheel in the bottom of the powdered chalk container. Keep dark-colored ones for marking on light fabrics and vice versa.

LIQUID FRAY RETARDANT

A drop or two provides a quick fix for raveling fabric and corners clipped too enthusiastically. It, too, should be tested first on a scrap.

POINT TURNER

This inexpensive gadget turns corners right side out neatly and without poking through the stitching line.

SPECIALTY PRESSER FEET

For most sewing machines it is possible to buy additional presser feet to handle all sorts of specialized sewing tasks. Those listed below are especially helpful for the projects in this book.

Walking or even-feed foot. This is a quilter's best friend; it's made to feed multiple layers of fabric evenly so that the edges are still aligned at the end of a long seam. It is also helpful for keeping plaid patterns matched along a seamline, and for sewing fabrics that scoot, such as velvet and corduroy.

Piping or cording foot. This one allows stitching very close to a cord, producing nice, tight piping.

Hemmers. These are handy for working narrow hems on ruffles and other long expanses of fabric. It takes a bit of practice to operate them efficiently, and it's worth the effort.

Applique foot. The foot is often made of clear plastic for better visibility. It exerts less pressure on the fabric so that the work can be turned without raising the presser foot.

Edge guide foot. It controls the fabric edge, permitting fast and accurate topstitching.

Embroidery foot. This one has a wider groove on the bottom to allow it to slide smoothly over densely stitched areas. Some are open at the front for better visibility.

Quilting foot. With one "toe" exactly 1/4" wide, it provides a perfect seam guide when patchwork instructions call for 1/4" seams.

Fabrics

Choice of an appropriate fabric for a decorating project is as important to the outcome as are good design and flawless workmanship. A fabric that looks sensational on the bolt may be all but impossible to sew, or might lose all its beauty in the first washing, or the pattern and color may prove overwhelming rather than breathtaking in the quantity required for, say, curtains.

CHOOSING FABRICS

When considering a fabric, try to picture it as the finished article. A slipcover, for example, requires a stable fabric with little stretch and with a fairly sturdy character. If it will be used in a family room or child's room, thought should be given to choosing a pattern and color that will camouflage spots. This fabric should be easy to wash and dry and require no more than token pressing.

It is important to know the fiber content of fabric chosen for a decorating project—whether it is cotton, wool, silk, polyester, or whatever. The fiber content determines how fabric will behave during construction, whether it is washable, whether it is likely to fade in sunlight, whether it will wrinkle terribly, and what its life expectancy might be. The fabric's weave structure or surface texture, such as gabardine, velvet, satin, etc., may be important aesthetically but is less of a practical consideration.

Fabrics should be labeled on the bolt as to fiber content and often with care instructions too. In mill-end and discount stores this is not always the case. If it is not possible to find out what the fabric is, wash or dry clean it before cutting to be safe.

Fabrics are divided into two broad categories according to their intended use: fashion fabrics for clothing, and decorator fabrics. Decorator fabrics are usually subjected to fairly heavy chemical finishing processes to give them stability and resistance to soil, water, sun fading, and stains. These fabrics must be dry cleaned to preserve the finishes and even then may lose their qualities over time. Fashion fabrics can certainly be used for decorating projects and may be a better choice if washability is an issue. Look for fabrics that are stable and not too delicate, and perhaps choose larger-scale patterns.

Most of the projects in this book are made up of cotton fabric, one of the best bets for decorating. Cotton is available in a vast range of weaves, thicknesses, colors, textures, and patterns to suit every taste and budget. It can be soft and drapey or firm and tightly woven. Most cottons are washable and many are relatively crease-resistant. Cotton is one of the easiest fabrics to sew and press, so it is an excellent choice for novice sewers.

PREPARING FABRIC FOR SEWING

A little preparation before cutting into the fabric can go a long way toward creating a successful project.

Preshrinking fabrics is essential if the finished article will be washed. Natural fiber fabrics, such as cotton or wool, are especially prone to shrinkage the first time they are washed. If they are preshrunk before sewing, though, the finished article can be washed successfully.

Preshrinking simply means washing and drying the fabric in the same way the finished article will be washed and dried. The fabric should then be pressed, ironing in the direction of the lengthwise grain so as not to stretch it.

Most of the components of the project should be treated the same way. An exception is fusible interfacings. These can be preshrunk by dunking them into warm water, folding gently into a towel to absorb excess water, then allowing to drip dry. Cotton piping cord should not be washed either; instead use polyester cording for piping on washable items.

If the finished article will be dry cleaned, it is sometimes wise to dry clean the fabric before cutting it. This is good policy in the case of discount-store fabric not labeled as to content or care requirements, or flea market and antique shop finds.

FABRIC GRAINLINES

The grain of the fabric plays an important role in the finished appearance of an article. Woven fabrics nearly always stretch considerably on the diagonal, or bias. There is less stretch on the cross grain—perpendicular to the selvage edges—and less still along the lengthwise grain.

Pieces of any garment or furnishing are cut with grainlines in mind. A piece that will hang, whether it's a skirt or a drapery, should be cut on the lengthwise grain of the fabric so it will not lose shape after hanging for a period of time. Pieces that benefit from slight stretch, such as piping and ruffles, look nice when they're cut on the bias.

With decorating projects, always cut major pieces with the straight grain of the fabric, or with the straight edges parallel with the threads of the fabric. Large pieces, such as major parts of a slipcover, should be cut with their north-south lines on the lengthwise grain.

When bias-cut pieces are needed, cut as close as possible to the fabric's true bias, at a 45-degree angle. Fabric cut slightly on the bias usually will have the necessary stretch for piping or a soft ruffle but will give a lumpy look to a piece which should be cut on the straight grain.

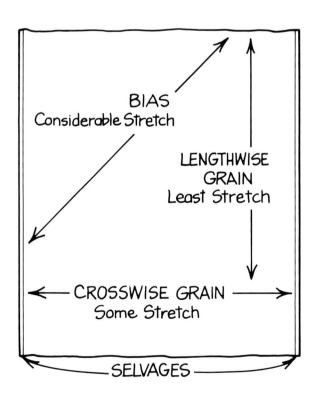

BIAS
Considerable Stretch

LENGTHWISE
GRAIN
Least Stretch

CROSSWISE GRAIN
Some Stretch

SELVAGES

STRAIGHTENING THE GRAIN

Often the printing or finishing process will pull a fabric askew. The result is that the lengthwise and crosswise threads, or grainlines, are no longer exactly perpendicular to one another. In large projects, such as draperies or slipcovers, the fabric won't hang straight.

To straighten fabric that is slightly off-grain, pull diagonally between the "shorter" corners to square it. For more serious cases, clip through the selvages near an end and pull a cross-grain thread to find the grainline. Repeat near the other end. Baste the ends together, steam the fabric, and pull slightly as described above. Smooth it out and allow it to dry. If it simply can't be squared, it is better not to use the piece for a large project.

Off-grain printing can be a problem too. Many printed patterns have a striped effect that will appear to run uphill or downhill if the fabric is cut, as it should be, with the grainlines. A decorator fabric with this problem may be stable enough, due to the finish it was given, that it can be cut with the pattern rather than with the grainlines and still hang correctly. Soft, unstable, or drapey fabrics printed off-grain should not be used for projects where grain of the fabric is important.

A short sewing primer

Space doesn't permit a complete course in sewing, but below are a few hints on good basic sewing practices that apply to any sewing situation.

BASICS

Always hold thread ends taut, to the back and slightly to one side, for the first few stitches to prevent bobbin jams.

As an alternative to backstitching, begin and end seams with 1/2" (1.5 cm) of very short stitches.

Always press a line of stitching to blend the stitches with the fabric, then press the seam open or press seam allowances to one side. Press every seam before sewing across it.

At corners, sew to within 1/2" (1 cm) of the corner, then shorten the stitch length. Instead of pivoting exactly at the corner, take one or two (depending on fabric thickness) short stitches on the diagonal. Then sew another 1/2" (1 cm) at the short stitch length and return the stitch length setting to normal.

Trim corners close to the stitching. If the fabric tends to ravel, with a short stitch length setting first sew around the corner a second time, just outside the first stitching line. Put a drop of liquid fray retardant on the corner stitching and allow it to dry before turning.

Grade seam allowances to prevent a visible ridge on the outside. Trim each seam allowance separately, leaving the one closest to the outer fabric the widest and trimming more from the innermost layer of fabric.

On seams with concave curves, clip through the seam allowance almost to the stitching so the seam allowances lie flat. Intervals between cuts will depend upon the depth of the curve and the flexibility of the fabric. For convex curves, cut V-shaped notches in the seam allowance so it will lie flat without ruffling when the piece is turned right side out.

To reinforce the seam and prevent stretching, staystitch seamlines at corners, curves, and at any point where the seam allowances will be notched or clipped. Before sewing the seam, sew along just outside the seamline in the seam allowance. Use the regular stitch or slightly shorter.

OVERCASTING AND FINISHING SEAMS

There is always the temptation among sewing perfectionists to make the inside look as good as the outside. This isn't always necessary or desirable. Overfinishing inside can create ridges along the seamlines that show through to the right side, especially after the article has been washed or pressed. Seams should be finished only when it's necessary to prevent raveling or when the inside of the article will show.

SPECIAL-PURPOSE SEAMS

Following are descriptions of several seams and seam treatments especially suited to decorating projects. It is a good idea to be familiar with them; they are all useful at one time or another.

French seams. This seam is a good choice for fabrics that ravel and for sheer fabrics. The raw edges are encased in the seam, resulting in a neatly finished wrong side. For a seamline with corners or with deep curves, this is not the best seam to use.

For a seam with 1/2" (1.5 cm) seam allowance:

1. With wrong sides together, stitch 1/4" (7 mm) from the raw edges.

2. Press stitching, and trim away half the seam allowances. Press seam allowances to one side. Fold exactly along the stitching line with right sides together. Press.

3. Stitch the seam again 1/4" from the folded edge.

Flat-fell seam. This durable seam is traditionally used in men's and women's tailored shirts. It is finished on both right and wrong sides, with the raw edges encased between lines of stitching. The flat-fell seam is ideal for bedspreads and similar articles where the wrong side is sometimes visible and which are subject to hard use or frequent laundering. The technique is most successful with seams that are straight or only slightly curved.

1. Stitch with wrong sides together, using the specified seam allowance. Press the stitching line, then press seam allowances to one side.

2. Trim the under seam allowance to 3/16" (5 mm). Fold under the raw edge of the upper seam allowance to the stitching line. Press.

3. Stitch close to folded edge.

Reinforced seams. When the wrong side of an article won't show but a strong seam is needed, this is a good technique.

1. Stitch with right sides together using the standard seam allowance. Press the stitching line.

2. If the fabric tends to ravel, overcast edges together.

3. Stitch the seam allowances together 3/16" from the seamline. Press to one side.

As an alternative, work the second line of stitching through all thicknesses and 1/4" from the seamline.

Serger seams. The serger's forte is the ability to stitch, trim, and overcast a seam with a single pass through the machine. It is a great time-saver for decorating projects. Keep the needle thread tension tight enough so that the seam doesn't pull loose and looper thread tension loose enough so that the edge lies flat.

Three-thread models should be used just to trim and overcast seam allowances, with the sewing machine used to sew the seam itself. The three-thread stitch is not strong enough to hold in woven fabrics.

PRESSING

Always press the stitching line before pressing a seam open or pressing seam allowances to one side. This causes the stitches to merge with the fabric to produce a smoother seamline. Always press a seam before sewing across it.

MAKING TIES

Fabric ties are wonderfully versatile closures for pillow covers, duvet covers, and slipcovers. They are easy to make of self fabric or can add interest when made in a contrasting color or material.

Cut ties on the lengthwise grain of the fabric. Use a 1/4" seam allowance at the long edges and at the end that will be finished, and the standard seam allowance at the end to be sewn to the article.

When a number of short ties are needed, it is sometimes quickest to make one long tube. Cut fabric double the desired finished width, plus seam allowances. Stitch the long edge with right sides together. Turn the tube right side out (a good tube turner is essential!), then cut it into sections. Turn one end of each piece to the inside and stitch across.

Very long ties are easier to sew right side out. Cut fabric twice the desired finished width and length plus seam allowances. Fold in half lengthwise and press. Then fold in the seam allowances at one end and on the long edges and press again. Stitch, with an edge guide foot if possible, close to both long edges and across the pressed end. Wider ties are fun to make using a different fabric for each side. For each fabric, cut a piece the desired finished width with seam allowances on all sides. Stitch the two, right sides together, along the long edges and across an end. Turn and press, and edgestitch if desired.

GATHERING

A few simple tricks can cut the tedium of gathering long stretches of fabric.

To gather a relatively short piece, such as a ruffle for a pillow, first loosen the upper thread tension slightly and use a stitch length just slightly longer than normal. Working on the right side of the fabric stitch two rows, spacing them 1/8" (3 mm) on each side of the seamline. Break the stitching at about the halfway point. Draw up both bobbin threads to gather the piece to the desired length.

For a long piece, such as the skirt on a slipcover or a dust ruffle, or when working with heavy fabric, use a length of gimp cord for gathering. Cut the cord slightly longer than the fabric. Set the machine for a fairly long zigzag stitch at medium width. Hold the cord taut just inside the seamline and stitch over it so the left swing of the needle penetrates the fabric at, or barely over, the seamline. Take care not to stitch through the cord. Draw up the cord to gather the fabric. After stitching, the cord can be removed and reused, or left in place to strengthen the seam.

RUFFLES

A neatly applied ruffle will soften the lines of a pillow or comforter cover. Ruffles add a distinctly feminine touch to the furnishings they decorate. Purchased trim, finished along both edges, gathered up and stitched along the edge of an article, makes a quick and easy contrasting ruffle. A matching ruffle can be made to measure from fabric scraps.

A fabric ruffle can be made with a single thickness of material that's hemmed at the outer edge and sewn into a seam. For a double thickness ruffle no hemming is necessary—the strip is folded lengthwise and both edges incorporated into a seam.

Use light- to medium-weight material to make a fabric ruffle. Fabric can be cut on the bias, especially for a doubled ruffle, for soft folds along the gathering line. Cut on the cross grain or lengthwise grain, the ruffle will be a little stiffer.

Cut fabric 1-1/2 to 2 times the length of the edge to which the ruffle will be applied. Use the greater length for thinner fabrics and very full ruffles; use less for heavy fabric. If the ruffle will be used on an edge with corners, as on a square pillow, use the greater length to allow enough fullness at the corners.

For the width of a single ruffle, determine the finished width and add seam and hem allowances. For a double ruffle add seam allowance at both long edges.

Use French seams to piece fabric strips if necessary to obtain the correct length. Join the ends if the ruffle will be continuous around an edge, or hem the ends. Hem the edge, if the ruffle is single thickness. A narrow hem presser foot is a great time-saver for this job!

For a double ruffle, piece the strips with a standard seam and stitch the ends as for the single thickness ruffle. Then fold the piece in half lengthwise, right side out, and press. Gather through both thicknesses. Mark matching points on the unfinished edge of the ruffle and on the edge to which it will be sewn; for example, mark both seamlines into quarters.

Gather the unfinished edge of the ruffle as described in the section about gathering fabric, above. Draw up the gathering threads just slightly tighter than seems necessary to fit the seamline onto which the ruffle will be sewn. Pin it right side up to the right side of the article, matching seamlines and raw edges. If there are corners, adjust the gathers so there will be more fullness at the corners. Pin the ruffle in place, pulling slightly along the finished edge so the gathers will be straight. Stitch.

HEIRLOOM SEWING

Heirloom sewing, or French "handsewing" by machine involves a few special techniques. The delicate laces and edgings used for these projects are embroidered on fine Swiss cotton batiste or made of very fine cotton thread.

The finishing process for these materials usually involves preshrinking, but as a precaution they should be washed before sewing. Use mild soap and wash them by hand, or put them into a lingerie bag and machine wash on the delicate cycle. Hang them to dry, then press. They are easier to work with if a little spray starch is used when pressing.

For heirloom sewing use a new, very fine machine needle, size 8/60 to 10/70. The size will depend upon the

2. Sewing entredeux. Trim away batiste from one side of the row of holes. Set the zigzag stitch length so that the needle goes into each hole in the entredeux. Place the entredeux and other fabric with right sides together, the entredeux on top, and the edges offset slightly so that the thick edges are not on top of each other. Set the stitch width to go just off the fabric edges on the right swing and into the holes on the left. Then trim and sew the other edge of the entredeux in the same way.

3. To sew two rolled and whipped edges together, offset the edges, and sew in the same way as for entredeux. Set the stitch width so the needle goes just over the fabric edges on the right swing and covers previous stitching on the left.

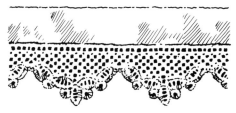

EDGING

INSERTION

ENTREDEUX

weight of the other fabrics in the piece. Use fine all-cotton thread, the size often designated "lingerie weight."

A special set of terms is used for the heirloom sewing materials:

Edging, as the name indicates, is meant to be sewn at the edge of a fabric. One edge of this trim is straight, the other irregular.

Insertion has two straight edges and is sewn between two fabrics or to other lace or edging.

Entredeux is a strip of regularly spaced embroidered holes stitched on cotton batiste. The word means "between the two" and it's used to join lace to fabric or to other lace. It also serves to strengthen seams. Some insertions are edged with entredeux.

HEIRLOOM SEWING TECHNIQUES

1. Unfinished edges (without entredeux attached) must be finished in order to strengthen seams between the delicate materials. This is done by a technique called rolling and whipping. Set the machine for a moderately short zigzag stitch. The stitch width should be slightly more than 1/8" (4 mm) so that the stitch will catch the fabric 1/8" from the edge on the needle's left swing and go off the edge on the right swing. The stitching will roll the edge, leaving it cleanly finished. For machines with variable needle position, the buttonhole foot can be used and the needle position changed accordingly so that the rolled edge is guided along one of the grooves in the bottom of foot.

Whether purchased or made to match, piping gives a professional-looking finish to pillows and other soft furnishings. It is almost always used for upholstery and slipcovers to give definition to the lines of the chair or couch. Piping can make a piece look "custom designed" rather than "homemade." Piping has its practical functions, too. It strengthens seams—important in upholstery and slipcovers—and it evens out seamlines that are less than perfectly straight.

Piping can be simply a narrow, folded strip of fabric sewn into the seam. More often the fabric is sewn around a cord to add dimension. A great range of commercially made decorative cords is available from home decorating suppliers; these have a narrow welt added so they can easily be sewn into a seam. Whichever the case, if the article to which the piping will be applied is going to be washed, then the piping must be preshrunk in the same manner as the other fabrics.

For custom-covered piping, cord can be purchased in a variety of sizes. Thicker cord exaggerates the seamlines on plump cushions; finer cord provides a more subtle finish for a small upholstered footstool or perhaps on a slipcover for a straight chair.

Piping cord is made of either cotton or polyester. Use polyester for washable items; the cotton does not hold its shape through laundering.

Fabric strips for piping usually should be cut on the true bias. This produces very flexible piping that can be sewn around curves and corners without puckering. Bias piping used with striped and plaid fabrics eliminates the need for matching at the seamlines. If the piece to be piped has only straight lines, and if the fabric stretches moderately on the cross grain, strips to cover piping could be cut this direction instead.

To determine the cutting width of the fabric strips, measure the diameter of the cord and add seam allowances at both sides, plus 1/8" to make up for width lost to bias stretch. It's easiest and most accurate to cut bias strips with a rotary cutter, ruler, and cutting mat. If the planned project requires yards and yards of piping, this might be the time to invest in these helpful tools.

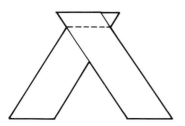

Join fabric strips to make up the needed length, as shown in the illustration. Press the seams open.

Fold the fabric strip snugly around the cord, right side out, with the fabric edges even. Use a zipper foot or cording foot to stitch as closely as possible to the cord without catching it in the seam.

To apply the piping, align the piping stitching line with the seamline of the main fabric and stitch along the piping stitching line. At the outer corners clip the piping seam allowances almost to the stitching. For inner, or concave, corners, cut V-shaped notches in the piping seam allowances so they will lie flat around the curve.

Where piping ends meet, there are two ways to provide a neat finish. One method is to bend the piping across the seamline and into the seam allowance as shown in the illustration. Then open the piping seam just to the seamline and clip out the excess cord.

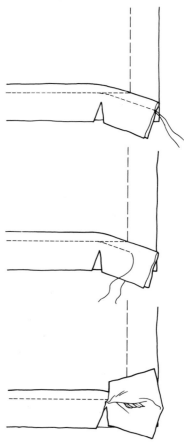

As an alternative, the ends of the piping can be abutted. Fold the ends of the covering to the inside, and clip away the extending bits of cord. Whipstitch the ends of the covering together by hand after the piping is sewn in place.

When the end of a piped seam will be hemmed, the piping should be tapered into the seam allowance just at the hemline to eliminate bulk in the hem. Trim away the cord below the hemline as described above.

Pillows and pillow covers

In this section are instructions for making the basic pillow styles that serve as starting points for the designs in this book. Each pillow has its own unique features that are described with the photo. Techniques and tips for the variations shown in the photographs—cording, ties, ruffles, and so on—are explained in the special techniques section beginning on page 12. For sewers with limited experience, it's a good idea to make a paper or muslin pattern for a design before cutting the decorator fabric.

FABRIC REQUIREMENTS

The best way to figure yardage requirements is to draw a diagram on graph paper. Measure a purchased pillow form as described in the instructions for the specific pillow style, below. Wrap the form with batting, if desired, before measuring. For a pillow made with loose filling, work from the proposed dimensions. Calculate fabric needed for trims—piping, ruffles, ties, and so forth. Allow extra, if necessary, to match plaids, bold stripes, or prints, particularly across the back opening.

Pillows and cushions look best when they're firm and plump, fitted snugly into their coverings. For this reason no ease allowance is added to actual measurements.

INSIDES

Ready-to-cover pillow forms can be purchased in a variety of shapes, sizes, and fillings. Foam pillow forms vary in density. For chair seat cushions, denser foam is a good choice so the cushion won't bottom out when sat upon. For seat-back cushions and decorative pillows, softer foam is adequate. Foam pillows can be made to look less stiff if the form is wrapped with a layer of batting and then sewed into a muslin liner before covering.

If a nonstandard shape or an unusual size is needed, an inner liner is made first and filled with feathers, down, kapok, foam chips, or fluffy synthetic fiberfill. The liner is made the same size as the outer cover and can be muslin or any inexpensive fabric, although if the pillow will be stuffed with down or feathers the liner fabric should be very tightly woven "downproof" cotton.

To make the liner, determine the finished dimensions of the pillow, add seam allowances, and cut a front and back. Sew the front and back together, shortening the stitch length somewhat around the corners and leaving an opening on one side for turning and stuffing. Clip the corners close to the stitching line; turn. Fill the liner, fold in the seam allowances along the opening, and stitch closed.

BACK OPENINGS AND CLOSURES

The addition of an opening along the back or side of the pillow cover takes just a little extra time and allows easy removal of the cover for dry cleaning or laundering. The kind of opening, and whether or not fasteners should be used, depends upon the pillow's function. A lapped opening without fasteners is suitable for decorative pillow shams in the bedroom, whereas cushions for much-used kitchen chairs might require heavy-duty zippers. Hook and loop tape, snaps, or snap tape also work well to secure the opening. Buttons and ties can perform as decorative elements of the design as well as functional closures.

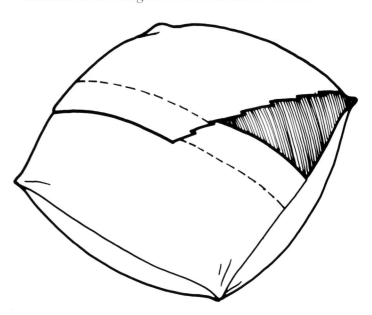

The opening should be large enough that the pillow can be removed easily from its cover. A pillow form made of dense foam may require a larger opening than will a loosely filled down pillow, for example.

On decorative pillows the opening can be located inconspicuously on the back, centered, or close to one edge. Box pillows often have a zipper along the welt, extending from one corner to the next or, on very large or firm cushions, across the back and around the two adjacent corners. For comfort's sake, openings on bed pillow covers are best placed at one end.

One of the simplest openings, often used on European-made pillowcases, is across an end. One cover section, either front or back, is lengthened and folded to the inside to form a flap. The inner edge of the flap is hemmed. The flap can also be a separate piece of fabric, a contrasting color, or perhaps a pattern. In this case, ties can be sewn into the seam and at the hemline of the other cover section in the corresponding positions.

To plan the back opening, make a paper pattern the size and shape of the cover front. Draw a line across the piece where the opening will be placed and cut the pattern on the line. Determine the seam and/or hem allowances needed for the kind of closures to be used and add the appropriate amount to each cut edge of the pattern before cutting the fabric. Stripes, plaids, and bold prints should be matched at the closure line. If the opening involves overlapped hemmed edges, match the pattern at the point where the fabric layers will meet, not at the cutting line.

For a zipper add a 1/2" (1.5 cm) seam allowance at each cut edge. Purchase a zipper approximately 2" (5 cm) shorter than the seam in which it will be inserted so that the ends of the seam can be stitched securely.

When using buttons, snaps, snap tape, or hook and loop tape, plan for an overlap slightly wider than the tape or the width of the buttons. Add 1" to 2" (2.5 cm to 5 cm) for a double hem along each edge to provide support for the fasteners. With light- to medium-weight fabrics, or fabrics that stretch, it is wise to add a strip of fusible or sew-in interfacing inside the hemmed edges for stability.

For pillow shams with no fasteners, allow an overlap of approximately 3" (7.5 cm) for a 14" (36 cm) pillow to 4" (10 cm) for an 18" (46 cm) pillow.

Make the back of the pillow (or whichever side has the opening) and attach the closures before assembling the pillow. Baste the back pieces together across the ends of the opening to keep them in place.

Knife-edge pillow

This pillow is flattened at the outer edges and thicker at the center. It is quick and easy to construct and can be made with a purchased form or with any filling material. Decorative cording, self piping, or a ruffle can be sewn into the edge seam. Any kind of decorative elements can be used on the front and back.

MEASURING AND CUTTING

Measure two adjacent sides of a rectangular form or determine finished dimensions of a filled liner. Add 1" (3 cm) to the length and width measurements for seam allowances. Cut a paper or muslin pattern to these measurements.

Adjust the corners for a better fit. Fold the pattern in half, then in half again, so that edges and corners are even. Mark a point about 3" (7.5 cm) from the corner on each side. Mark a point 1/2" (1.5 cm) in from the corner and equidistant from the sides. Round off the corner slightly, then taper to each marked point as shown. Recut the pattern. Use this pattern to cut the pillow front, or top, and for the back if there will be no back opening. Cut the liner, too, if loose filling will be used.

For the back or underside, mark and cut the pattern where the opening will be. Add hem and seam allowances according to the style of opening that will be used, as described above.

CONSTRUCTION

1. Assemble the back according to the kind of opening used. Baste sections together across the ends of the opening in the seam allowances.
2. Apply piping, ruffle, or other decorative trim to the pillow front. (Specifics are given in the section called "A short sewing primer," beginning on page 12.)
3. Stitch the back to the front. If there is no back opening, leave a section of the seam open to insert the pillow.
4. Reinforce all corners on the front and back. Stitch about 3" (8 cm) around each corner with a short stitch length, stitching just outside the seamline in the seam allowance. Trim corners. Turn right side out and press.

Knife-edge pillows with borders

A flange around the edge of a knife-edge pillow creates a frame or border. It can be an extension of the cover front or back, or it can be a separate piece, perhaps in contrasting fabric, sewed around the perimeter. The width of the border should be in keeping with the size of the pillow: 2" to 3" (5 cm to 7.5 cm) for a small to average pillow, 4" or 5" (10 cm to 12.5 cm) for a larger pillow.

Simple bordered pillow

The border on this pillow is an extension of the cover itself, delineated by topstitching or a narrow applied trim.

MEASURING AND CUTTING

Measure the pillow as for the knife-edge pillow above. Add to each edge the desired finished width of the border plus 1/2" (1.5 cm) seam allowance. Use these measurements to cut the cover front or top and for the liner if one will be used. Measure for the back according to the kind of opening that will be used as described on page 17.

CONSTRUCTION

1. Assemble the back according to the kind of opening used. Baste sections together across the ends of the opening in the seam allowances.

2. With right sides together stitch front to back. Leave an opening on one side if the cover has no back opening on the back. Trim corners, turn, press.

3. With chalk or a fabric marker draw the stitching line for the border. Stitch, again leaving an opening if necessary.

4. Insert the pillow. Turn in seam allowances at the outer edge opening; press and stitch. Stitch the remaining border section.

Knife-edge pillow with double border

This border consists of two layers of fabric, separately hemmed, with neat-looking mitered corners.

MEASURING AND CUTTING

Measure the pillow form or filled liner as for the simple flanged pillow above. To the finished dimensions add two times the finished width of the border plus seam allowance at each edge.

Use these measurements to cut the front or top of the cover. If there will be an opening on the back, determine the placement and type of closure to be used, then add seam and/or hem allowances at the opening as described on page 17.

CONSTRUCTION

1. Make the cover back according to the kind of opening being used. Baste the sections together across the ends of the opening in the seam allowances.

2. Fold under and press the hems on the front and back. The hem is the width of the finished border plus seam allowance.

3. Miter the corners: Open out the fold at each corner and refold on the diagonal, placing the new fold exactly across the intersection of the creases formed by the first folds and aligning the foldlines adjacent to the corner. Then fold in again on the original foldlines, making sure the diagonal folds just meet.

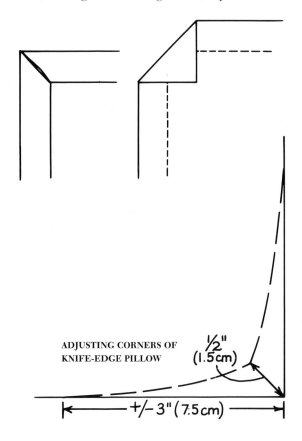

ADJUSTING CORNERS OF KNIFE-EDGE PILLOW

1/2" (1.5 cm)

+/- 3" (7.5 cm)

4. Pin or baste the front to the back, wrong sides together, with chalk-mark stitching lines for the border. Topstitch through all thicknesses. If there is no back opening, leave the seam open along one side, insert the pillow, then finish topstitching.

Knife-edge pillow with contrasting border

Strips of border fabric are sewed to the edges of the cover front and back, their corners mitered, and the cover assembled like the simple flanged pillow.

MEASURING AND CUTTING

For the central part of the cover measure the length and width of the pillow form and add 1" (3 cm) to each measurement for seam allowances. Cut the front. If there will be a back opening, determine the placement and type of closure to be used, then add seam and/or hem allowances at the opening as described on page 17.

Decide the finished width of the borders and add 1" (3 cm) seam allowances. For length, use the measurement for that side of the pillow and extend each end by the finished width of the border plus 1/2" (1.5 cm) seam allowance. For example: If the pillow is 12" (30 cm) square and the finished border will be 2" (5 cm) wide, strips for the border would be cut 3" (7.5 cm) wide and 17" (43 cm) in length. Cut two strips (front and back) for each edge.

CONSTRUCTION

1. Assemble the central section of the cover back according to the kind of opening being used. Baste across the ends of the opening in the seam allowances.
2. On the central front and back pieces mark the point at each corner where the seamlines intersect. Mark the midpoint of each side.
3. Mark the midpoint of each border strip.
4. Stitch a border strip to each edge of front and back, with right sides together, matching the midpoints and starting and ending the stitching exactly at the marked corner points.
5. Miter all corners: Fold the piece in half diagonally, right sides together. Stitch from each marked corner point to the outer edge of the border.
6. With right sides together, stitch front to back, leaving an opening for turning if the back cover has no opening. Turn.
7. If the back cover has no opening, insert the pillow at this point. Carefully align the border seamlines; pin or baste. Topstitch around the cover on the border seamline.

Box pillow

Box pillows may be round or square or can be shaped to fit a chair seat. They are flat across the surface and have an inset strip, a welt or "boxing strip," around the perimeter. Openings on box pillow covers are most often along the back of the welt so the pillow can be used with either side up. Cord or piping often is sewn into the edge seams to give these pillows a finished look.

MEASURING AND CUTTING

To cover a rectangular pillow, measure two adjacent sides and add 1" (3 cm) to each measurement for seam allowances. The total of all four side measurements is also the finished length of the side welt.

For a round pillow place the form on a sheet of paper and draw around it, then add 1/2" (1.5 cm) seam allowance all around. Carefully measure the inner line to determine the finished length of the welt strip.

Decide the width of the welt. Width should be in proportion to the size of the pillow, approximately 2" (5 cm) for a small pillow to perhaps 4" (10 cm) for a fairly large one. If a pillow form will be used, simply measure its thickness.

Determine the length of the opening. It should be large enough that the cover can be removed easily from the pillow form. A cover for a sturdy foam form will probably need a larger opening than a cover for a soft, down-filled cushion. On a square cushion the opening usually extends almost all the way across the back edge; on other styles it may extend around the back corners just into the side welts. On a round cushion it may be approximately 1/4 to 1/3 the circumference of the cover, depending upon the stiffness of the cushion.

Subtract the length of the opening from the total finished welt length as measured above; this will be the length of the remaining welt section. Add 1" (3 cm) to the length and to the width for seam allowances.

For the section of the welt with the opening, divide the welt width measurement in half lengthwise and add a seam/hem allowance at the inner edges according to the kind of closure to be used. Add 1/2" (1.5 cm) at the outer edges of both pieces for seam allowances and add 1" to the length of both pieces.

CONSTRUCTION

1. Install a zipper or other closure in the appropriate welt section, then join to the other welt section at the ends, right sides together.
2. If piping will be used, stitch it to both cover sections. Instructions for making and attaching piping are on page 16.
3. Working from the original finished measurements, mark a point on each edge of the welt to correspond to the pillow corners. Staystitch about 2" (5 cm) along the seamline at each marked point.
4. With right sides together stitch the strip to one cover section, matching the marked points to the corners and clipping to staystitching at corners. Stitch the welt to the other cover piece in the same way.

Bolster, neckroll, and duffel pillows

These cylindrical pillows are often used at the ends of a couch or exhibited decoratively on a bed.

BASIC CONSTRUCTION

Bolster pillows can be made with purchased forms or with any kind of filling. A bolster pillow also can be made quickly by rolling up a piece of thick fiberfill batting, jelly roll fashion, and stitching a muslin cover around it.

The ends of this cover can be made in several different ways. The cover can simply be extended lengthwise and gathered up at the center on each end. It can be lengthened even more and each end knotted to keep the pillow in place. The ends can be separate rectangular pieces sewed to the cylindrical part of the cover then pleated or gathered up at the center. Another option is to sew fitted circular end pieces in place for a smooth, tailored pillow.

A cover that is open at one or both ends can be removed easily for laundering. For other styles a zipper can be installed in the lengthwise seam.

MEASURING

For any of the bolster pillow styles, measure or calculate the finished length and circumference of the pillow. Measure or calculate the diameter (the circumference divided by 3.14159. Remember pi?). Seam and hem allowances will depend on the style selected, below.

Bolster pillow with set-in ends

The ends of this pillow are separate rectangular pieces, gathered or pleated at the center of each end. Piping may be sewn into the end seams for a professional finish. The inner edge can be left unfinished, or hemmed and drawn up with a ribbon or gathered and then covered with a button.

MEASURING AND CUTTING

For the main cover cut one piece: in width, the circumference of the pillow plus 1" seam allowances; in length, the length of the pillow plus 1" seam allowances. Cut two end pieces the width of the main cover; in length, the radius of the pillow plus 1/2" (1.5 cm) seam allowance. Also add hem allowance if the center will be hemmed to make a casing for a gathering cord.

CONSTRUCTION

1. Stitch the lengthwise edges of the main piece, right sides together, to form a tube. If a zipper will be used, install it in this seam.
2. Stitch the end pieces together in the same way. If the ends will be gathered at the center, sew a line of gathering stitches or hem one end of each piece to insert the cord.
3. Stitch piping around the ends of the main tube, if desired. Instructions for making piping are on page 16.
4. Stitch the ends to the central tube with right sides together. Clip seam allowance as necessary; turn.
5. Insert the pillow. Gather or pleat at the center of each end. If the edges are unhemmed, stitch to secure.

Bolster pillow with flat ends

This cover fits smoothly over the pillow form or liner. The ends are cut to fit without gathering or pleating. A zipper in the lengthwise seam allows easy removal of the cover.

MEASURING AND CUTTING

Cut the main piece: in length, the length of the pillow plus 1" seam allowances; in width, the circumference of the pillow plus 1". Cut two circles for ends, each the diameter of the pillow with 1/2" (1.5 cm) seam allowance added around the outer edge.

CONSTRUCTION

1. Stitch the lengthwise edges of the main piece, right sides together, to form a tube. Install a zipper, if used, in this seam.
2. Sew piping to the edges of the tube, if desired. (Instructions for making piping are on page 16.)
3. If piping is not used, staystitch around each end of the tube on the seamline.
4. With right sides together, stitch the end pieces to the tube, clipping almost to the staystitching or piping stitching line as necessary to achieve a smooth fit.

Duffel pillow

Like bolster pillows, duffel pillows are cylindrical in shape. This pillow cover is made from a single piece of fabric gathered at the ends. The edges can be hidden by a decorative button where they meet at the center or they can be hemmed and drawn up with a pretty ribbon or cord.

CUTTING

Cut one piece: in width, the circumference measurement plus 1" (3cm) for seam allowances; in length, the length of the pillow plus the diameter. If the gathered edges will be hemmed to form the casing for a gathering cord, add two times the desired hem allowance.

CONSTRUCTION

1. Stitch the lengthwise seam, right sides together, to form a tube. Install a zipper in this seam if desired. For hemmed ends leave an opening just outside each hemline to insert the drawcord.
2. If the ends will be left unfinished, work gathering stitches at each end, 1/4" (1 cm) from the edge (see page 14). For hemmed ends, fold, press, and stitch hems in place.
3. Gather up one end, insert the pillow, then close the other end. Sew on buttons if desired.

Duffel pillow with extended ends

The cover is lengthened at the ends, then tied with ribbons or fabric ties. The ends can be hemmed or faced with matching or contrasting fabric.

CUTTING

Cut one piece: in width, the pillow circumference measurement plus 1" seam allowances; in length, use the pillow measurement and add for each end the radius of the pillow, the desired finished length of the extension, and a hem allowance. (Or a seam allowance if a separate facing will be used.) Cut two facings, each the width of the main piece and the length of the extension plus allowance for a single hem.

CONSTRUCTION

1. Hem one end of each facing, if used, then stitch one to each end of the main piece with right sides together.
2. Stitch the long edges, right sides together, to form a tube, stitching the facings and main piece in one continuous seam. Turn facings to the inside.
3. Hem the ends if facings are not used.
4. Center the pillow in the tube and tie the ends.

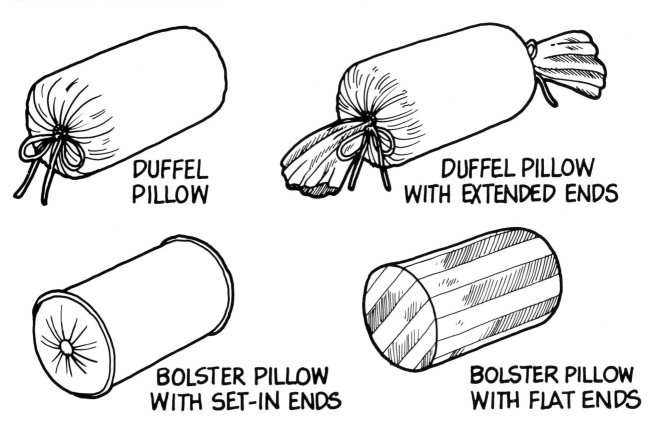

DUFFEL PILLOW

DUFFEL PILLOW WITH EXTENDED ENDS

BOLSTER PILLOW WITH SET-IN ENDS

BOLSTER PILLOW WITH FLAT ENDS

Duvet Covers

The best fabric choice for a comforter cover is washable cotton or a cotton blend. Wide cotton sheeting is available by the yard in a range of colors. Two different fabrics might be incorporated, perhaps comfortable cotton flannel for the underside of the cover and a decorative fabric on top, or a solid color and a print just for variety. Be sure to preshrink all fabrics to prevent problems resulting from the fabrics shrinking at different rates.

BASIC DESIGN

The covers shown in the photographs all have openings across the lower edges and are made in one of two ways: envelope-style, with either the front or back extended at the open edge to create an inward-folding flap, or with a separate facing sewn around the opening. The envelope style is easier to make and can be made from a single piece of fabric. With a separate facing ties can be sewn into the seam, and the facing itself can be made of a complementary fabric if desired. If a ruffle or other trim will be added around the edges, the facing provides a seam at the lower edge into which the trim can be sewn.

Duvet cover with end flap

The flap is an extension of the underside of the cover, folded inward and sewn into the side seams. Buttons or hook and loop tape strips can be sewn to the flap near the foldline, with buttonholes or the other tape pieces in the corresponding positions along the hem of the upper cover.

MEASURING AND CUTTING

Use the comforter measurements to determine the finished dimensions of the cover. Add 6" (15 cm), or as desired, for the finished length of the flap. Where a seam allowance is required, use 1/2" (1.5 cm).

To the finished measurements add seam allowances at both sides and at the upper edge of both pieces. On the upper cover piece add 1-1/2" (3.5 cm) for a 1" (2.5 cm) finished double hem. Cut one.

On the under section of the cover add 6" at the lower edge plus 1" (2 cm) for a narrow double hem. Cut one.

If it is necessary to piece the fabric to obtain the desired finished width, use a full fabric width at the center and the narrower pieces at the sides. Remember to add seam allowances for the piecing seams.

To make the cover from a single piece of fabric, just eliminate seam allowances at the upper edge. In this case it is wise to topstitch the completed cover close to the upper edge foldline to help keep the comforter in place.

CONSTRUCTION

1. If buttons or hook and loop tape closures will be used, fuse or baste a strip of interfacing to the wrong side along the hem of the cover top. Fuse another strip to the facing on the cover under section, along the foldline.
2. Stitch hems at the lower edge of the cover top section and at the inner edge of the facing on the under section.
3. Pin the cover sections with right sides together, aligning the upper edges and sides. Align the hemmed

lower edge of the upper section with the facing foldline of the under section. Fold the facing along the foldline up over the upper cover section; pin at the sides. Stitch the sides and upper edge.

4. Work buttonholes along the hem of the upper cover section and sew buttons in corresponding positions on the facing, or sew on hook and loop tape.

Duvet cover with faced opening

A ruffle, piping, or other trim can be basted to the upper section of the cover and then sewn into the seams. Tie closures can be sewn into the facing seams, or buttons or hook and loop tape can be added, as described above. Detailed instructions for making and sewing piping are on page 16, for ruffles see page 14, and for ties see page 13.

MEASURING AND CUTTING

Measurements for this cover are calculated in the same way as for the cover with the end flap, above, except that seam allowances are added only at the lower edge of each main piece.

Two facing pieces are cut to the width of the main section, and 7-1/2" (18.5 cm) in length, for a finished facing 6" long. Cut ties if desired.

CONSTRUCTION

1. Stitch facing sections with right sides together at both sides. Stitch a 1" (2 cm) double hem around one edge.
2. If a trim is used, pin or baste it to the right side of the upper cover section.
3. Pin the cover front to the back. Stitch the sides and the upper edge.
4. Pin tie sections to the right side of the upper cover section along the lower edge and in corresponding positions on the under section.
5. Pin the facing to the cover with right sides together. Stitch.
6. If buttons or hook and loop tape closures are used, stitch as for the cover with end flap.

CHAPTER 1

Sweet Dreams

Pink *and* white bedroom

A luxurious bedroom look is often simple to achieve with a well-coordinated stack of pillows. The pink stripe print on the duvet cover works well with solids, similar stripes, and florals.

DUVET COVER

Materials

- Cotton fabric, according to measurements

Construction

1. Refer to the duvet cover instructions on page 24, taking note of the details in step 2.

2. Cut the facing as a separate piece, then stitch around the open end with the ties in place.

ASSORTED PILLOWS

Materials

- Fabric
- Pillow form or stuffing

Construction

Refer to the basic cutting and assembly instructions on pages 17 and 18.

Bedroom comfort

An intriguing mix of patterns and colors adds instant life to a drab room. The delicate white pillows are a nice counter to the bold plaids. The red and white comforter uses low-loft batting for lightweight comfort and is embellished with large, machine quilted squares. The blue and white comforter uses a high-loft batting and is embellished with several concentric lines of stitching inside the perimeter, then a pattern of diamonds for the center.

The chair cover requires only a moderate amount of fitting, making it a reasonable project for a novice. The cover is suitable for a chair with fairly straight lines; very narrow piping around the seat and back defines the chair's silhouette.

Materials

- Cotton fabric, according to measurements
- Low-loft batting

Measuring and Cutting

Determine the finished size for the comforter and cut the batting to these measurements. Add seam allowances on all the edges and cut the fabric front and back.

Construction

1. Stitch the cover, right sides together, leaving an opening to insert the batting. Trim the corners, turn, and press.

2. Insert the batting and stitch across the opening. Pin, then machine stitch a large pattern of squares.

BLUE AND WHITE COMFORTER

Materials

- Fabric, according to measurements
- High-loft batting

Measuring and Cutting

Determine the finished size for the comforter and cut the batting to these measurements. Add seam allowances on all the edges and cut the fabric front and back.

Construction

1. Stitch the cover, right sides together, leaving an opening to insert the batting. Trim the corners, turn, and press.

2. Insert the batting and stitch across the opening. Pin, then machine stitch the pattern, referring to the illustration as a guide. When doing the machine quilting, try to plan so that the stitching is not always in the same direction. Start, perhaps, by stitching the pattern lines that form a large X across the face of the quilt to anchor the layers together.

WHITE PILLOWS

Materials

- Fabric
- Pillow form or stuffing
- Eyelet edging (optional)

Construction

1. Refer to the basic cutting and assembly instructions on page 17, taking note of the details in steps 2 and 3.

2. For the eyelet-covered pillow, cut a ruffle double the perimeter measurement of the pillow. Finish it on one side with a narrow double hem, then sew it into the front/back seam.

3. For the solid white pillow, sew a commercially made eyelet edging into the seam.

Materials

- Fabric, according to measurements
- Piping or piping cord
- Closures (hook and eye or hook and loop tape, fancy buttons, etc.)

Measuring

It is helpful—and less confusing—to draw a diagram and record the measurements in the appropriate places.

A. Chair back, from midpoint of side rail around the back to the midpoint of the other side rail. Make separate measurements at the top and at seat if width varies.

B. Height of chair, from the top center back to the floor. For a curved back, as in the chair shown in the photograph, measure at the center and at the sides.

C. Height of back, from the top of the seat. Measure for a curved back as above.

D. Top of the seat to the floor.

E. Height of the seat: top of the seat to the bottom of the seat.

F. Bottom of the seat to the floor.

G. Width of the seat. If the front and back width differ, measure both.

H. Depth of the seat, from the front to the back.

I. Circumference of chair at base of seat, including legs.

Cutting

For novice slipcover-makers and for chairs with odd curves and angles it is a good idea to cut the pieces slightly larger than the measurements for those areas that require fitting, then pin or baste them on the chair before final stitching. Use a 1/2" (1.5 cm) seam allowance unless instructions indicate otherwise.

Inside back: Use measurements A and C, add seam allowances on all sides and cut one. Mark the centers of all edges.

Outside back: Use measurements A and C. Cut separate left and right pieces, adding for hems and underlap: on the right side add 2-1/2" (6.5 cm) at the center back; on the left side add 4-1/2" (11 cm)

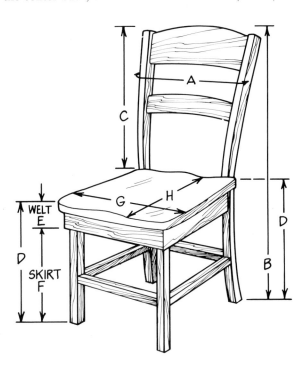

at the center back. For both pieces add seam allowances on all other edges. Mark center of each outer edge.

Seat: Use measurements G and H, add seam allowances at all edges, cut one. Mark the corners, center front, and back.

Welt: Use measurement I for circumference, adding hem/underlap allowances at the center back opening as for the outside back. For length, or height, use measurement E or as desired. Add seam allowances at both long edges; cut one. Mark the front and back corners, center front, and center back.

Skirt: Use 1-1/2 times measurement I for the circumference, adding hem/underlap allowances at the center back as above. For the length, use measurement F or as desired, making sure that the finished welt and skirt lengths won't exceed measurement D. Add a hem allowance at the lower edge and seam allowance at the upper edge; cut one. Mark the center backs.

If piping will be used, allow enough length for the inner/outer back seam and in both the upper and lower welt seams. Cut the fabric this length to cover the piping cord. Complete instructions for making and sewing corded piping are on page 16.

Construction

1. Stitch the piping to the inside front, beginning and ending at the lower edge seamline.

2. Hem the inner edges of the back pieces by folding the raw edge 2-1/2" (6.5 cm) to the wrong side; press. Fold under the raw edge 1/2" again; press and stitch close to the fold or work a hand or machine blind hem.

3. Overlap the hemmed edges of the outer back, placing the foldline of the right side at the center back. Match the front for size. Baste together in seam allowance.

4. Stitch the seat section to the inner back, right sides together, matching centers and beginning and ending stitching at the side seamlines of the seat. (The side seamlines of seat will not meet the back seams.)

5. Stitch the outer to the inner back with right sides together, matching centers. Stitch with the front uppermost, stitching on the piping stitching line.

6. Stitch the piping to the right side of the welt upper and lower edges. Begin and end the piping at the center back.

7. Hem the lower edge of the skirt. Work a gathering stitch along the upper edge from the center back to the center back. Adjust the gathers to fit the welt. Stitch.

8. Stitch the welt/skirt to the seat, matching the center fronts and back edges. Finish the center back edges f the welt/skirt as for the upper back. Attach closures as desired.

Blue *and* white bedroom

Fine embroidered Swiss cotton edging and insertion combined with ginghams and solid-colored cottons create an elegant bedroom ensemble. Working with the embroideries calls for some special sewing techniques – heirloom sewing – described on page 14. Heirloom sewing techniques work best with soft all-cotton or lightweight linen fabrics rather than cotton/synthetic blends.

Materials

- Main fabric for pillowcase back and front
- Soft cotton accent fabric for front trim and piping
- Embroidered insertion
- 1/8-inch (3 mm) piping
- Fine cotton sewing thread for insertion stitching
- Buttons

Construction

1. Measure and cut the fabrics as described on page 16. At the piecing seams across the pillow front—where the insertion will be placed—add only 1/8" for seam allowances. Along the open end of the front add a fairly wide hem allowance so that the button-holes can be worked on the hem. (The added layer of fabric will serve as reinforcement.)

2. Cut out the piping strips, referring to the basic instructions on page 16. Be sure to cut the strips on the crossgrain, rather than on the bias since the crossgrain works better with the heirloom finishes. Cut two 1-1/4" wide (3 cm) strips that are the length of the pillowcase's short end. Fold the strips in half lengthwise, right side out, and stitch 1/8" from the fold. Trim seam allowances.

3. Blind hem the open edge of the front trim by hand or machine, then work the buttonholes.

4. Roll and whip the edges of all pieces that will be involved in the piecing seam: main fabric, accent fabric, insertion, and piping.

5. Assemble the front, stitching one piece to another as described in the Heirloom Sewing instructions. Hem the back flap, then sew the cover front to the back, referring to the instructions on page 18 if necessary. Sew on buttons.

Materials

- Blue and white cotton fabrics
- Scrap of interfacing or tear-away backing
- Fine sewing thread for edging stitching
- Swiss edging

Construction

1. Measure and cut the pillowcase as the one above, but add full seam allowances for the main section/trim seam. Don't add a hem allowance at the open end.

2. Roll and whip the long edges of the accent piece and trim. Sew on the trim, referring to the Heirloom Sewing techniques. Work the buttonholes, reinforcing behind each with a small piece of firm interfacing or tear-away backing. Sew the accent piece to the main front section, then assemble the pillow as described on page 18.

Materials

- Main fabric, according to measurements
- Contrasting checked fabric, according to measurements
- Solid color fabric, according to measurements
- Rickrack
- Embroidered Swiss insertion
- Buttons

Measuring and Cutting

Measure your blanket or comforter and use these measurements as finished measurements for the cover. For the cover top's width, measure the width of the insertion and subtract 1/8" (3 mm) on each side of each narrow strip for finishing/seam allowance. Allow the same amount at the piecing seams of the fabric widths. At the outer edges of the cover, add 1/2" (1.5 cm) seam allowance. In length, add 1/2" (1.5 cm) seam allowance at the bottom and 1-1/2" (4 cm) hem allowance at the top.

For the cutting length of the cover's main bottom piece, subtract 7-1/2" (18.5 cm) from the finished length measurement. In width, add 1/2" (1.5 cm) at each side for seam allowances.

The cutting size of the solid-color border across the top will be the width of the main bottom section, and 17" (43 cm) in length. Cut 2 pieces this size. For the contrasting trim, cut a strip the length of the border width, and 4" (10 cm) wide. Cut rickrack this same length.

Construction

Read about heirloom sewing, pages 14-15, for complete instructions on the special techniques used in working with Swiss embroideries.

1. Piece the cover top. Roll and whip the fabric edges and insertion strips involved in the piecing seams. Assemble the top. Hem the upper edge. Turn under 1-1/2" (4 cm), then turn the raw edge under 1/2" (1 cm). Press and stitch.

2. Fold the trim for the upper border in half lengthwise, right side out. Center the rickrack over the folded edge and stitch. Pin the trim to the right side of one border piece. With right sides together stitch this piece to the other border section along the long edge to which the trim is pinned. Turn and press. Baste the border sections together along remaining raw edges.

3. To determine placement of buttonholes, place the border, right side up, on the cover top with the sides even and the raw edge of the border extending 8-1/2" (21.5 cm) beyond the hemmed edge of the cover. Mark the buttonholes along the border edging above the insertion strips on the cover top. Work the buttonholes, reinforcing behind each with a small piece of tear-away stabilizer.

4. Stitch the border to the cover bottom section along the upper edge. Position the cover top and bottom with right sides together. Fold the border extension to the wrong side so that the fold is even with the hemmed edge of the cover top. Stitch the sides and lower edges. Turn; press. Turn the border over the hemmed edge of the cover front.

5. Mark positions for the buttons. Fuse or stitch small pieces of firm interfacing to the wrong side of the insertion strips at the marked positions; sew on buttons.

Materials

- Pillow form or stuffing
- Checked fabric, according to measurements
- Embroidered insertion

Measuring and Cutting

Determine the finished size of the pillow, without ruffle. The seam/finishing allowance is 1/8" (3 mm) for the ruffle/edging seam and for seams both sides of the insertion on the pillow front. For other seams use 1/2" (1.5 cm) seam allowance.

Determine the style and location of pillow back opening (see page 17). Add seam and hem allowances and cut the back pieces.

For the front, calculate the finished size of the central panel, the outer border, and the insertion. For cutting length of the four outer borders and insertion strips, add twice their combined finished width, plus 1" (3 cm) for seam allowances, to the finished width of the central panel.

Cut a ruffle strip 1-1/2 times the finished perimeter measurement of the pillow, and to the desired width plus 1/2" seam allowance on one edge only. Cut the embroidered edging to the same length. The pillow shown is 18" (46 cm) square, with a 3" wide (8 cm) ruffle.

Construction

1. Assemble the pillow back according to kind of opening used. Roll and whip the long edges of the insertion pieces, one long edge of each border strip, one long edge of the ruffle, the unfinished edge of the edging, and around the perimeter of the central panel.

2. With right sides together, stitch an insertion strip to each border strip along the finished edges. Stitch the insertion edge of the border strip to each side of central

panel. Begin and end the seam at the point where the seamlines intersect at corners. Miter the corners of the border (see page 19, step 3).

3. With right sides together, stitch the edging to the finished edge of the ruffle. Sew the ends together. Fold the ruffle into fourths and mark the unfinished edge at each fold. Gather the unfinished edge of the ruffle. With right sides together and raw edges aligned, pin the ruffle to the cover front, matching the marks to the corners and adjusting the gathers for more fullness at the corners.

4. Stitch the cover front to the cover back with right sides together, keeping the ruffle free. Trim the corners, turn and press.

HEIRLOOM SEWING

The beautiful trims used in these projects are finely embroidered Swiss cotton batiste. Because they are somewhat fragile, some special sewing techniques are helpful when working with them. Insertion, used between two pieces of fabric, has two straight edges which usually require finishing before the strip is joined to fabric. Edging has one unfinished straight edge and one decoratively finished edge. As the name implies, it is used to trim the edge of a fabric.

A fine machine needle, size 8/60 to 10/70, is a necessity. It must be in perfect condition to ensure good stitching on delicate fabrics. Fine all cotton thread, often labeled "lingerie weight," produces a nearly invisible line of stitching and reduces puckering.

Raw edges of the trims should be finished using a technique called "rolling and whipping" before seams are sewn. This strengthens the seams and provides a cleanly finished edge. To do this, first set the machine for a zigzag stitch with a width of about 1/8" (3 mm) and a short stitch length. Position the fabric so that the needle penetrates the fabric a scant 1/8" on the left swing and goes just over the edge on the right swing. The stitching will roll the edge neatly. For bias-cut fabric or curved edges, stay stitch first with a fairly short stitch inside the seam allowance.

If your sewing machine has variable needle positioning, the buttonhole foot may be used instead. Change the needle position accordingly so that the rolled edge is guided through the groove on the bottom of the foot.

To sew two rolled and whipped edges together, offset the edges slightly so that one is not directly atop the other (to prevent an uneven line). Use a zigzag stitch with approximately the same settings as for rolling and whipping. Set the stitch width so the needle goes just over the fabric edges on the right swing and covers previous stitching on the left.

Pillow assortment

Homespun-style cotton fabrics in a variety of patterns work well together. You can add coordinating style to a simple wool blanket with a border of blanket stitches worked in colorful crewel yarn.

Materials

- Main and contrasting fabrics
- Piping (optional)
- Pillow forms or stuffing

Construction

1. Refer to page 17 for basic cutting and assembly instruction for the knife-edge pillows. Consider cutting your fabrics on the bias for added visual interest.

2. The large pillow, cream-colored cotton fabric with a leafy green print, has an easy-to-make self-border. Instructions on page 19.

3. For the standard bed-size pillows, cases with end flaps were made according to the instructions on page 18.

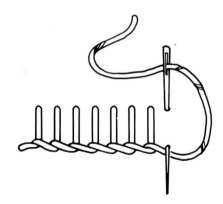

Ruffles *and* Lace

Soft cotton lawn makes a wonderful fabric choice for pillow shams: it's comfortable and airy and easy to work with for embroidery. The cotton plisse blanket cover was trimmed in a lacy edging to match some pillows. Ruffles for the pillow shams were embellished with machine-embroidered scallops.

BLANKET OR DUVET COVER

Materials

- Fabric, according to measurements
- Lace or eyelet edging 2" (5 cm) wide
- 8 mother-of-pearl buttons, 3/4" (2 cm) diameter

Construction

This cotton plisse cover is made according to the instructions for the duvet cover with end flap, page 24. Cut the edging 1-1/2 times the perimeter measurement, then gather it onto the cover top before the top and bottom are sewed together. Close the opening along the lower edge with the buttons.

Materials

- White cotton lawn fabric
- Cotton machine embroidery thread to match fabric
- Lightweight tear-away stabilizer, approximately 1 yd. (1 m)
- Sewing machine with embroidery functions

Measuring and Cutting

Measure and cut the fabric for the ruffle's pillow cover according to the instructions for the knife-edge pillow on page 18.

For the ruffle, cut a strip 6-1/2" (18 cm) wide and 1-1/2 times the pillow's perimeter measurement in length.

Construction

1. Make a paper pattern for the scallop design. Find a round object the diameter of the desired scallop width. Cut a strip of paper, such as adding machine tape, 1/4 as long as the ruffle if possible. Close to one end and one edge of the paper, draw halfway around the circular object to make a single scallop. Carefully fold the paper, accordion-style, making the folds exactly at the ends of the scallop. Cut along the scallop outline.

2. Smooth the paper and use it to outline the scallops along the edge of the ruffle. Cut the stabilizer into strips slightly wider than the depth of the scallops, then place them under the fabric edge for embroidery, adding strips as needed.

3. Stitch the marked line with a moderately short straight stitch. Trim away the fabric and stabilizer, cutting a scant 1/8" (3 mm) outside the stitching. Using the machine's embroidery foot and a satin stitch setting, stitch over the straight stitch lines, overcasting the fabric raw edge at the same time. Carefully tear away the excess stabilizer.

4. Assemble the pillow according to the knife-edge pillow instructions, but do not hem the ruffle.

Materials

- Fabric
- Pillow form or stuffing

Construction

This pillow is made according to the instructions on page 19 for the pillow with extended border, but the cover front and back are sewn with right sides together, then the edges finished with the embroidery as described above.

Curtains
with tab ties

Very clever and functional! These are the simplest possible curtains to make and, as window treatments go, require minimal fabric. This curtain is unlined to let light through.

Materials

- A length of 1" x 2" (2.5 x 5 cm) board, cut to window's inside frame width measurement
- Fabric and lining, according to measurements
- Tacks and tack hammer or staple gun

Measuring and Cutting

The finished width of the curtain will be the width of the window inside the frame. Measure for finished length from the upper front edge of the mounting board to the bottom of the window at the sill. The finished length of the ties is the same as that of the curtain; cut their width to 3" to 4" (8 to 10 cm), depending upon the curtain's width.

Cut the curtain 3" wider than finished width measurement, and 4-1/2" (12 cm) longer than the finished length measurement. Cut the ties 2-1/2" (5.5 cm) longer than the finished length measurement. In width, cut them twice desired finished width plus 1" (3 cm).

Construction

1. Paint or finish the mounting board as desired. Affix supports for the board to the inner frame of the window. With the board in place, doublecheck the curtain's length measurements.

2. Hem the bottom of curtain by folding and pressing 3" from the lower edge, then folding under the raw edge 1/2" (1.5 cm). Press and stitch. Hem the sides by folding the edges in 1-1/2" (4 cm) and then 1/2" (1 cm). Press and stitch.

3. Make four ties by folding a strip in half lengthwise with right sides together. Stitch the long edge and across one short end with a 1/2" seam. Trim, turn, and press. Topstitch the long edges and across the closed end.

4. Pin the ties at the top of the curtain (see photo), one of each pair on the curtain's right side and one directly behind it on the wrong side. Align the upper raw edges and baste. Turn under the top edge of the curtain 1/2", then press and stitch.

5. Position the curtain on the mounting board with the hemmed upper edge on top of the board 1" back from the board's front edge. Staple or tack along the top of the board. Replace the board on its supports. Tie the ties together around the lower edge of the curtain to hold it at desired height.

Materials

FOR EACH PILLOW

- Pillow form or stuffing
- Cording, optional

Construction

1. These pillows are made from the basic pillow instructions beginning on page 17. The floral print knife-edge pillow is made of bedspread fabric, trimmed with a hemmed single-thickness ruffle that's sewn into the edge seams. The white embroidered pillow with rose gingham ruffle is made the same way.

2. The pale striped pillow is in the knife-edge style too but with the border, in plaid fabric to match the curtains, made separately and sewn around the perimeter. The red corded piping defines the seamline.

3. The white pillows with an embroidered motif on a corner also are the knife-edge variety. The border on these is created by cutting the cover larger than the pillow, sewing the front to the back around the outer edges, then topstitching to center the pillow and create the border.

Materials

- Fabric, according to measurements

Construction

1. With giant yellow checks on the top and smaller checks underneath, this duvet cover is simple to make, with an opening across one end and no closures. Refer to page 24 for complete measuring and assembly instructions.

Materials

- Fabric, according to measurements
- Piping cord

Measuring and Cutting

Calculations are for a double bedspread and will require alteration to fit other bed sizes. The finished top measurements are 54" X 75" (137 X 190 cm). The finished length, or drop, is measured from the upper edge of the mattress to the floor and will depend upon bed height.

The top section requires 2-1/8 yds (2 m) of 55" (138 cm), or wider, fabric. For narrower fabric, twice the length will be needed in order to piece the top. If piecing will be necessary, use the full width of fabric at the center and add pieces of equal width at both sides. Remember to add seam allowances for the lengthwise seams

The skirt requires 15-1/2 yards (14-1/2 m) of fabric width. To calculate the yardage needed, measure the drop and add 1/2" (1.5 cm) seam allowance at the upper edge and 1-1/2" (4 cm) for a double hem around the bottom. The fabric width will dictate the number of pieces needed to make up the skirt width. Be sure to add seam allowances for piecing the seams.

For the piping, allow the length of the bed plus the width. Complete instructions for making covered piping are on page 16.

Construction

1. For the top, trim or piece the fabric to 55" X 77" (138.5 X 195 cm). This allows for 1/2" seams around three sides and a 2" (4 cm) double hem across the top.

2. Cover the piping cord and stitch the piping to the top, tapering into seam allowances at the upper hemline. Stitch lengthwise seams in skirt, and hem the lower edge with a hand or machine blindstitch.

3. To pleat the skirt, crease the fabric on the right side beginning 6-1/2" (14 cm) from one end on the right side and fold a 6" (8 cm) pleat. Fold another 6" pleat in the other direction so that the creases meet on the right side to form a box pleat. Pin. Measure 7" (18 cm) along the skirt and make another box pleat.

4. Repeat until there are 11 pleats. The 11th will be on the corner at the foot of the bed. Leave a 6" (15 cm) space and make the next pleat. Resume the 7" spacing and make a total of 7 pleats (excluding the corner pleat) across the foot. Leave a 6" space again and make the other corner pleat. Then pleat the remaining side to match the first, leaving 6-1/2" between the last pleat and the end of the skirt.

5. Baste the pleats in place on the seamline and again close to the edge of the fabric. With right sides together stitch the skirt to the top, matching the corners. Hem the top edge of the main section and ends of skirt.

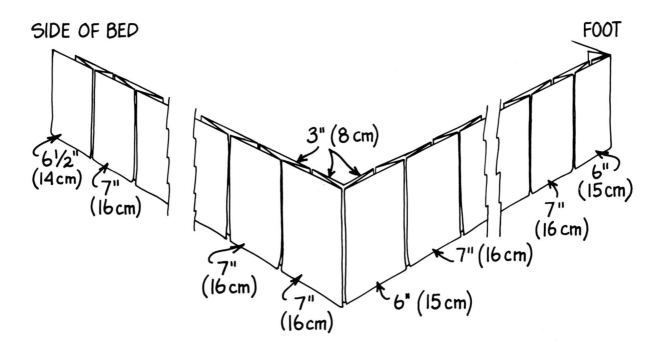

SIDE OF BED   FOOT

6½" (14cm) 7" (16cm) 3" (8 cm) 7" (16cm) 7" (16cm) 6" (15 cm) 7" (16 cm) 6" (15cm) 7" (16 cm)

Child's kingdom

The decorative curtain and valance provide a wonderful tentlike environment for kids' play. Affixed to the frame with adhesive-backed hook and loop tape, the projects are simple to make and easy to remove for laundering or a quick change of decor. The well-crafted bed pillows lend an air of distinction to the room.

Materials

- Fabric, according to desired finished size of valance
- Adhesive-backed hook and loop tape 3/4" (2 cm) wide

Measuring and Cutting

To determine the width and drop length of the strips, measure the bed frame from corner to corner. Add 1" (2.5 cm) at each short end and at the lower long edge for double hems. At the upper edge add 1-1/2" (4 cm). Cut pieces as needed.

Construction

Fold the upper edge 1/2" (1.5 cm) toward the right side; press and stitch. Stitch or press the hook and loop tape close to the fold along the upper edge. Press the corresponding lengths of tape to top of the bed frame.

Materials

- Fabric, according to measurements
- Adhesive-backed hook and loop tape
- 1" wide (2.5 cm) twill tape, approximately 3 yds. (2.5 m)

Measuring and Cutting

For the finished length, measure from the upper edge of the canopy frame to the floor and add 12" (30 cm) or desired amount. To this measurement add 1/2" (1.5 cm) for a single hem at the top and 4-1/2" (11 cm) for a double hem at the bottom. Allow a full width of 54" to 60" (137 to 155 cm) fabric for each panel.

Construction

1. Hem the sides of each panel: Fold the fabric 1-1/2" (4 cm) to wrong side; press. Fold under raw edge 1/2"; press and stitch. Stitch a double hem at the lower edge of each panel.

2. At the upper edge of each panel press 1/2" toward the wrong side. Work two rows gathering stitches, 1/4" and 3/4" (1 cm and 2 cm) from the fold. Cut pieces of twill tape to the desired gathered width of the panels plus 1" (3 cm). Fold ends under 1/2" (1.5 cm); press. Gather the panels to fit the tape. Position the tape strip on the wrong side of the panel to cover the gathering stitch lines. Stitch the tape to the panels along both long edges and across both ends.

3. Stitch or press one side of the hook and loop tape to the twill tape on panels. Press corresponding strips close to the top of the bed frame.

Materials

- Fabric
- Inset of fine needlework
- Backing material (if doing machine embroidery)
- Pillow form or stuffing

Construction

1. Refer to the basic cutting and assembly instructions for bordered pillows on page 19.

2. Separate the pillow casing from the border with a line of satin stitches, then finish the outer edge with a blanket stitch. (If embroidering by machine, be sure to use a backing material behind the outer fabric to prevent puckering.)

Materials

- Fabric
- Pillow form or stuffing

Construction

1. Refer to the basic cutting and assembly instructions for simple knife-edge pillows on page 18 and for ruffle making on page 14.

2. Cut the ruffle 1-1/2 times the pillow's perimeter measurement and hem the outer edge with a narrow double hem. (*Note*: The pillow in this photo features an extra-wide ruffle.)

Materials

- Fabric, according to measurements
- Buttons in assorted colors

Construction

Refer to the cutting and assembly instructions for a basic duvet cover, page 24 Close the end with an assortment of multi-colored buttons.

Materials

- A sturdy cardboard box with attached one-piece top
- White glue and brush
- Fabric, according to measurements
- Medium-weight fusible interfacing with little or no stretch, enough to back all fabric pieces
- Craft knife
- Rotary cutter, mat, and ruler are handy but not essential

Construction

1. Read through the directions for each section and calculate the total amount of fabric required. Fuse interfacing to fabric before cutting or as each piece is cut, taking care to avoid fraying the edges.

2. For the bottom, cut the fabric approximately 1/4" (1 cm) smaller than the box measurements. Spread glue thinly and evenly over the bottom of the box. Allow it to dry slightly until it is tacky, then press the fabric in place, smoothing it from the center to the outer edges in the direction of the fabric grain.

3. For the outer lid, measure the width and depth (front to back) of the box lid. Add 2" (5 cm) to the width and 4" (10 cm) to the depth, then cut the fabric to these measurements. Apply glue to the outer box lid, its edges, and about 3" (7 cm) below the lid along the upper back of the box. Allow the glue to dry slightly, as above. With the lid closed, place the fabric onto the lid so that it extends about 1" (2.5 cm) beyond the front and sides and about 3" down the back. Clip the back corners to fit if necessary. Smooth the fabric into place.

4. For the inner lid, measure as for the outer lid. Add 3" to the depth measurement and cut the fabric. On the sides and front edge fold the fabric 1/2" (1.5 cm) to the wrong side; press. Miter the corners: Open out the fold at each corner and refold on the diagonal, placing the new fold exactly across the intersection of the creases formed by the first folds and aligning the fold lines adjacent to the corner. Then fold in again on the original fold lines, making sure the diagonal folds just meet. Press. Glue the hems in place using the glue sparingly. Allow to dry.

Spread glue onto the inside of the lid to within 1/2" of the outer edges, all the way to the back (hinged) edge and about 3" down the inside of the back. With the box lid opened back, position the hemmed inner lid fabric with the hemmed sides equidistant from the side and front edges and the unhemmed edge down into the back of the box to form the inner section of the hinge.

5. For the outer sides, measure the outer perimeter and height. Add 1" to the perimeter measurement and add 2" to the height. Cut the fabric to these measurements. Glue

1/2" hem at one short end (the overlap) and along the upper long edge as described above.

Hem the back upper edge. Determine the placement of the fabric: Start at the back about 1" from a corner with the unhemmed end of the piece and wrap it around, keeping an even 1" extension of fabric above the top of the box. Clip the fabric 1" in from the edge at back corners. On the hemmed end, glue 1" hem along the top from the clip to the hemmed end. At the unhemmed end cut away the 1" hem allowance along the top from the clip to the end of the piece.

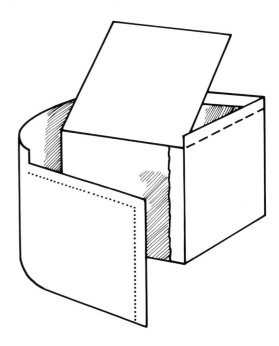

6. Spread glue around the sides of the box, along the upper edges, and for about 1" around the top inside. Press the fabric in place, wrapping it exactly as for hemming the back edge, above. Spread a little glue along the fabric at the beginning end to hold the overlapping end. Turn the box upside down. Fold the corners as for mitering and trim them neatly. Glue around all the edges.

7. For the inner sides, measure the inner perimeter and height. Add 1-1/2" (4 cm) to the height measurement and 1" to the perimeter, then cut the fabric. Spread glue around the inside of the box to within 1/4" of the top and around the edges of the bottom for about 1". Wrap the fabric, starting and ending as for the outer covering and positioning the upper hemmed edge evenly 1/4" down from the top.

8. For the inner bottom, measure the interior width and depth. Add 1/2" to each measurement and cut out the fabric. Glue a 1/2" (1 cm) hem around the edges, mitering the corners. Spread glue onto the box bottom to within 1/4" of the sides. Press the fabric in place.

Pink *and*
green nursery

Coordinating cotton prints provide a fresh look
for baby's room. The matching crib bumper provides soft padding and is a good place to showcase a small bit of needlework.

Materials

- Fabric for patchwork, approximately 1/2 yd (.5 m) each of 4 fabrics
- Fabric for backing and borders, 1-5/8 yds (1.5 m) 54" (137 cm) or wider (twice this amount for narrower fabric)
- Cotton flannel for interlining, 1-5/8 yds 36" (90 cm) or wider
- Rotary cutter and mat
- Quilters' pins or safety pins
- Even-feed or walking presser foot

Measuring and Cutting

Wash and dry the cotton flannel at least twice to preshrink it, and the patchwork fabric at least once.

Cut the back and interlining 52" x 35" (164 cm x 107 cm). Cut strips for borders: two at 55" x 4" (146 cm x 10 cm); two at 38" x 4" (100.5 cm x 10 cm).

Determine the placement of the different fabrics, referring to the diagram as a guide. Cut the patchwork pieces in the following sizes and quantities:

A. Cut 42, 9-1/2" x 3-1/2" (25 cm x 9 cm)

B. Cut 8, 6-1/2" (16 cm) square

C. Cut 10, 12-1/2" x 3-1/2" (33 cm x 9 cm)

D. Fold piece B in half diagonally and add a 1/4" (.5 cm) seam allowance at the diagonal line, then cut six from this shape.

Construction

1. Piece the larger squares and triangles as shown in the diagram, using exactly 1/4" seam allowance. Then assemble the blocks. The outer edges will be uneven.

2. Layer the backing and the patchwork, right sides out, with interlining between. Pin the layers together.

3. If desired, machine quilt the layers together by stitching along some or all of the patchwork stitching lines. An even-feed or walking presser foot will help keep layers from shifting.

4. Trim the patchwork even with the backing and interlining. (There is 1/2" (1 cm) seam allowance at outer edges.) Baste the layers together just outside the seamline. Mark the center of each border strip and each side of the quilt. On the quilt corners mark the point at which the seamlines intersect.

5. Sew the border strip to the right side of the quilt, with right sides together. Use 1/2" (1.5 cm) seam allowance. Match the centers and begin and end the stitching at the marked corner points. Miter the corners as described on page 19. Turn under raw edge on back so fold just covers previous stitching line. Baste. On the right side stitch along the border seamline.

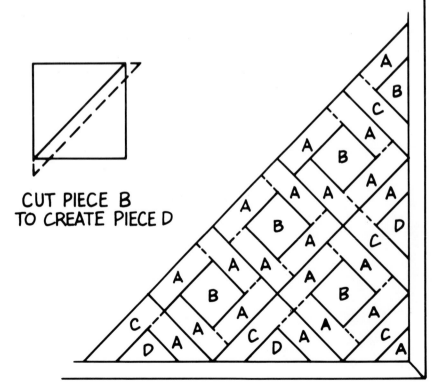

CUT PIECE B
TO CREATE PIECE D

Materials

- Cotton or cotton blend fabric, according to measurements
- Thick fiberfill batting, according to measurements
- Double-fold bias tape, according to measurements
- Small needlework piece or decorative motif cut from a complementary fabric, if desired.

Measuring and Cutting

Measure the inner width of the crib's headboard for the main section of the bumper. Determine the width for the end extensions. For the length, measure from the lower point of the crib rail to a point approximately 2" (5 cm) below the top of the mattress. Cut the batting to these measurements, one piece for the main section and one for each end.

Cut the cover fabric as a single piece. Add a 1/4" (.5 cm) seam allowance around the outer edges. Cut one front and one back.

Construction

1. Stitch the appliqué to the inner main cover section, if desired. Layer the fabrics, right sides out, with the batting centered between. Stitch close to the outer edges with an open zigzag stitch at medium width. Define the joints between the main section and the ends with lines of straight stitch.

2. For the ties, cut 16 pieces of bias tape 12" (30 cm) long. Press under the raw edge at one end of each. Stitch the end and along both long edges.

3. Position pairs of ties on the cover, one tie on the front and one on the back, with the unfinished ends at the fabric edge. Place a pair at the upper and lower corners at each end, and at the upper and lower edges at the stitched joint. Baste them in place, then fold the bias tape over the cover edge and stitch in place.

FLORAL BORDERED SHEETS AND TOWELS

Materials

- Towels with plain border strips at the ends and/or plain white sheets
- Fabric scraps

Construction

1. Wash and dry the towels, then measure the border. Add 1/2" (1 cm) to all edges and cut the fabric strip. Press under the seam allowances and sew to the towel, stitching close to the fold.

2. Decorate plain white sheets as you did in step 1. For the crib sheet in the photo, stitch a strip of rose-printed cotton along the hem of the sheet.

DUVET COVER AND FABRIC BOOK COVER

For the duvet cover, refer to the instructions on page 24 and use a row of mother-of-pearl buttons across the opening to keep the cover in place. For the book cover, refer to the instructions on page 133, but choose a single floral print and dainty ribbons.

White nursery

Delicate cotton dotted Swiss is a wonderful fabric to use in the nursery. It's dainty in appearance and easy to care for. The bassinet skirt is really a simple curtain, joined at the sides and gathered to fit around the top of the frame.

As an option to framing the baby's needlework gifts—a cross stitch alphabet from grandma or a trapunto sampler from Aunt Sue — use them to make pillow covers to carry out the nursery's all-white theme.

BASSINET FRAME LINER

Materials

- Fabric, according to measurements (wrong side will show)
- Double-fold bias tape, 1/2" to 3/4" (1.25 cm to 2 cm) wide and the length of the pieced fabric widths
- Ribbon, 1/4" (1 cm) wide and the length and the circumference of the bassinet plus approximately 24" (60 cm)
- Bassinet with frame

Measuring and Cutting

Measure the height of the bassinet's frame to determine the fabric's length. Add 14" (36 cm) for the outer ruffle and tuck-in. For width, use 1-1/2 to 2 times the circumference of the frame. Allow more fullness for lighter fabrics, less if the fabric is stiff or heavy.

Construction

1. Piece the fabric to obtain the necessary width, using French seams (page 12). Join the two sides to make a wide tube. Hem the upper and lower edges with narrow double hems.

2. Mark a placement line for the bias tape 5" (12.5 cm) below the upper edge, on the wrong side. Work two buttonholes along the placement about 1" (2.5 cm) apart.

3. Cut bias tape the width of the fabric plus 1". Press open the center fold. Center the tape over the placement line, beginning on one side of the buttonholes and ending at the other. Fold under the tape ends at the beginning and end, then stitch very close to both folded edges.

4. Arrange the fabric over the frame with the casing approximately 1" below the upper edge. To gather the fullness, thread the ribbon in through a buttonhole, through the casing, and out through the second buttonhole.

Materials

- Two-sided fabric, according to measurements
- Double-fold bias tape
- Ribbon, 1/4" wide
- Bassinet with curtain frame

Measuring and Cutting

Suspend a flexible tape measure from the top of the frame to determine the curtain's length. Allow it to drape freely and measure to a point below the bottom of the bassinet. Add for a narrow double hem at the upper edge and approximately 2" (5 cm) at the bottom. For width, plan the curtain to be the circumference measurement of the bassinet or slightly wider.

Construction

1. Piece the fabric widths if necessary, using French seams (page 12). Hem the sides with narrow double hems, then hem the top and bottom.

2. Apply bias tape casing across the piece as described above, folding under the tape ends at the fabric edges. Thread a ribbon through the casing to gather the curtain over the frame.

Safety Note: Once the infant begins to grab at objects, the bassinet curtains will need to be removed.

COVERLET

Materials

- Soft, all-cotton fabric, according to measurements
- Cotton flannel, according to measurements
- Washable or disappearing fabric marker

Construction

1. Refer to the measuring and assembly instructions on page 24. Preshrink the fabrics.

2. Draw stitching lines on the cover using a ruler and washable fabric marker. Stitching with a walking or even-feed foot will prevent shifting of the fabric layers.

3. Parallel rows of straight stitch 3/8" (1 cm) apart give the appearance of trapunto quilting but are fast and easy to work. On the coverlet in the photograph the design consists of concentric squares, a simple and attractive pattern.

Plaid bedroom

The fresh, cool look of this room is achieved with simple bed curtains. The curtains are made from six panels, each made of a single width of fabric hemmed on the sides and bottom and faced along the upper edge. Bed frames can be purchased ready-made or built by your fav-orite wood-working enthusiast.

An attractive bedspread doubles as a warm cover for chilly nights. For this cover the same fabric was used for both sides, but with a solid-colored fabric on one side the cover could be reversed to change the look of the room. A double layer of cotton flannel inside gives the cover its cozy quali-ty. Cotton flannel tends to shrink a good bit, so buy extra length then wash and dry the fabric two or three times before cutting. Old flannel sheets would work well, too.

Materials

- Fabric, according to measurements
- Fusible interfacing

Measuring and Cutting

For curtains that will close fully along the sides of the bed select fabric at least 45" (115 cm) wide for a standard twin or double bed and at least 54" (137 cm) for extra-long bed sizes. To determine the finished length, measure from the desired upper point of the curtain to the floor. To this length add 1/2" (1.5 cm) for an upper seam allowance and 2-1/2" (6 cm) for a double hem at the bottom.

For the facing at the top of each panel, cut one piece the width of the panel and 3" (8 cm) wide. Cut a strip of lightweight fusible interfacing for each facing, 2" (5 cm) long and the width of the facing.

Use a flexible tape measure to determine tab length. Measure from the desired top point of the curtain, over the frame, and back to the starting point. Add 1" (3 cm) for seam allowances to figure the cutting length for each tab. For finished tabs 2" wide, cut fabric strips 5" (13 cm) in width. It is easiest to sew tabs as one continuous piece, if possible, then turn right side out and cut to the tab lengths. In the design shown each panel has eight tabs.

Construction

1. Fuse interfacing to the wrong side of each facing piece, centering it between the upper and lower seamlines. Follow the manufacturer's instructions as to iron setting and moisture requirements.

2. Make the tabs by folding the fabric pieces in half lengthwise and stitching the long edges. Turn right side out, press, and cut to individual tab lengths.

3. Press the lower edge of each panel under 2-1/2" for a hem, then turn under the raw edge 1/2" (1 cm) and press again. Stitch with a machine blind hem or straight stitch close to the inner fold.

4. Position the tabs across the top of the curtain. Fold the tabs in half and align the unfinished ends with the curtain's edge. Place a tab at each side with its outer edge 2" in from the curtain's edge. Space the remaining tabs evenly across panel and baste them to the curtain in the seam allowance.

5. With right sides together stitch a facing section to the top of each curtain with 1/2" (1.5 cm) seam. Press the seam allowances toward the facing.

6. To hem the sides, turn the edges 2" to the wrong side; press. Turn under the raw edge 1/2" (1 cm); press. Stitch as for the bottom hems, breaking the stitching at the facing seamline to keep the tabs free.

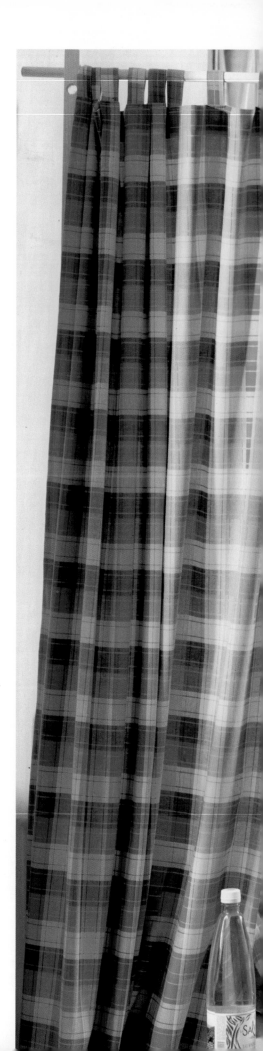

Materials

- Fabric, according to measurements
- Cotton flannel, according to measurements

Measuring and Cutting

Determine the finished size of the cover and add seam allowances on all sides.

Construction

1. If necessary, piece the fabric widths, using a full width at the center and narrower pieces along both sides.

2. Place the top and bottom fabrics with right sides together, then position flannel on top. Stitch around the edges, leaving an opening on one side for turning. Turn and press; stitch across the opening. Topstitch 1/4" (.5 cm) from edges.

Materials

- Fabric
- Pillow form or stuffing
- Narrow piping (for bolster pillows)
- Zippers (for bolster pillows)

Construction

1. Refer to the instructions on page 16, noting the following details. The shams have a 4" (10 cm) border with a lapped opening across the back. The sham on the bench is similar, but uses a 2-1/2" (6.5 cm) self border.

Designer Note

Fabric-covered shades give the room a professionally decorated look and aren't at all difficult to make. Kits, with roller, hardware, and fabric backing, can be purchased where decorating fabrics are sold or from home supply stores. Follow the manufacturer's instructions.

Materials

- Sturdy cotton or linen with little or no stretch, according to measurements
- Firm woven interfacing (necessary only if you choose a fabric with stretch)

Measuring and Cutting

Remove and measure the existing seat fabric to determine dimensions. Because the old fabric probably has stretched it should be stretched taut across the stool before final measurements are taken. Add 1-1/4" (3 cm) allowance for double hems across the upper and lower edges of the piece. Add allowance for a single hem at each side. If interfacing will be used, cut it the same size.

Construction

1. If interfacing will be used, hem it as one with the outer fabric.

2. Tack or staple the hemmed cover in place across one side of the stool. Pull the fabric evenly taut and tack it to the other side. Tack the ends first, then the center, then add subsequent tacks between centers.

Bed curtains

Don't be intimidated by the expensive look of this bed-room. Bed frames can be purchased as stock items or can be custom made in a weekend by a reasonably handy person. Check woodworking magazines for design choices and instructions. On the frame shown, the upper rails are removable so the curtain tabs can be slipped over them. For a frame without this feature the tabs can be made slightly longer, with one end sewn into the facing seam and the other finished and equipped with some sort of fastener.

Materials

- Lightweight fabric, according to measurements (cotton lawn makes a good choice for its softness and light-diffusing quality)
- Lightweight fusible interfacing

Measuring and Cutting

For curtains that will close fully along the sides of the bed select fabric at least 45" (115 cm) wide for a standard twin or double bed, at least 54" (137 cm) for extra-long bed sizes. To determine the finished length, measure from the bottom of the curtain frame to the floor. The tops of the curtains will be below this point, allowing several inches of the curtain length to drape on the floor. To this length add 1/2" (1.5 cm) for upper seam allowance and 2-1/2" (6 cm) for a double hem at the bottom.

For the facing at the top of each panel, cut one piece the width of the panel and 3" (8 cm) wide. Cut a strip of lightweight fusible interfacing for each facing, 2" (5 cm) long and the width of the facing.

Use a flexible tape measure to determine tab length. Measure from the desired top point of the curtain, over the frame, and back to the starting point. Add 1" (3 cm) for seam allowances to figure the cutting length for each tab. For finished tabs 2" wide, cut fabric strips 5" (13 cm) in width. (It is easiest to the sew tabs as one continuous piece, if possible, then turn right side out and cut to the tab lengths.) In the design shown each panel has eight tabs.

The tiebacks should be long enough to tie comfortably around the bed frame and two curtain panels. The ties in the photo were cut on the crossgrain of 45" (115 cm) fabric, so each tie is 44" (111 cm) long. The finished width is 6" (15 cm), so they were cut 7" (18 cm) wide to allow for seam allowances.

1. Fuse the interfacing to the wrong side of each facing piece, centering it between the upper and lower seamlines. Follow the manufacturer's instructions as to iron setting and moisture requirements.

2. Make the tabs by folding each piece in half lengthwise and stitching the long edges. Turn right side out, press, and cut to individual tab lengths.

3. Hem the lower edge of each panel. Press under 2-1/2", then turn under raw edge 1/2" and press again. Stitch with machine blind hem or straight stitch close to the inner fold.

4. Position tabs across top of each curtain. Fold tabs in half with unfinished ends aligned. First place a tab at each side with its outer edge 2" in from the curtain edge and tab ends aligned with top of curtain. Space remaining tabs evenly across panel. Baste tabs to curtain in the seam allowance.

5. With right sides together stitch a facing section to the top of each curtain with 1/2" seam. Press the seam allowances toward the facing.

6. Hem the sides by turning the edges 2" to the wrong side; press. Turn under the raw edge 1/2" and press. Stitch as for bottom hems, breaking the stitching at the facing seamline to keep the tabs free.

White bedroom

A covering of lightweight cotton plisse protects blankets and comforters in winter and makes an attractive coverlet for summer. Blanket covers are usually made just slightly larger all around than the blankets beneath them. Note that the interest in this room comes from the wonderful textural variety in the all-white fabrics.

BLANKET COVER

Materials

- Fabric, according to measurements

Measuring and Cutting

Measure the length and width needed for the finished cover. Add 1" to 2" (2.5 to 5 cm) for the hems at the sides, top, and bottom. (Most fabrics will have to be pieced to get the necessary width.) If the chosen fabric is too narrow, buy twice the required length. Use one length for the center portion of the cover. Add seam allowances and cut pieces of equal width from the second length, then sew them to either side.

Construction

Use flat-fell seams (page 13) for the piecing so the cover will be reversible. Clip through the selvage every inch or two before seaming or hemming so that the shrinkage that usually occurs along the selvages won't cause puckering along the seams and hems. Hem the edges.

DUFFEL PILLOW WITH KNOTTED ENDS

Materials

- Lightweight fabric such as cotton lawn or batiste, according to measurements
- Inner pillow*

*The pillow will show through, so it should be somewhat attractive in itself or covered before beginning the project.

Construction

Make the cover like the duffel pillow with extended ends, page 22. Cut the extensions 25" (63.5 cm) longer than the pillow at each end to allow for the knot, and add a narrow hem.

BOLSTER PILLOW WITH EYELET TRIM

Materials

- Fabric
- Narrow satin ribbon
- Eyelet edging

Construction

1. This delicate bolster pillow is made like the bolster pillow with extended ends, page 22, with the ends gathered and tied with narrow ribbon. The rectangles for the ends are cut, in length, to the radius of the pillow plus about 10" (25 cm) to allow for narrow hems and a nice fullness to the tied extensions.

2. Double the pillow's circumference and cut the eyelet edging to this measurement. Stitch the ends of each piece together with an overcast or French seam. Gather the unfinished edges of the eyelet and sew them to each end of the main cover piece with the wrong side of the ruffle to the right side of the cover. Then sew on the end pieces and hem the raw edges.

RUFFLED SHAM

Materials

- Fabric
- Eyelet edging

Construction

1. This elegant ruffled sham is made according to the instructions for the basic knife-edge pillow on page 18, using the sham opening. Cut the eyelet edging to twice the length of the pillow's perimeter. Join the ends with a French or overcast seam.

2. Gather the unfinished edge and draw up the gathering threads to fit the cover. Stitch to the cover front with the wrong side of the ruffle against right side of cover.

EYELET-TRIMMED DUVET COVER

Materials

- Fabric
- Eyelet edging
- Fusible interfacing
- Buttons

Construction

1. Make the cover according to the instructions on page 24, with a facing at the open lower edge of the top. Cut the eyelet edging to 1-1/4 times the perimeter measurement of the top, then sew it into the seam all the way around the pillow, gathering the edging heavily at the corners and slightly along the straight edges.

2. Apply fusible interfacing to the wrong side of the cover top facing and to the wrong side of the bottom flap to provide reinforcement under the buttons and buttonholes.

Colorful comfort

The comforter and quilted bedspread in this room both feature reversible sides, the comforter with red checks on one side and blue checks on the other, the bedspread with red and white checks on top and blue and white checks on the reverse. With both pieces reversible, changing the room's decor is as simple as remaking the bed. Details, such as the contrasting piping and quilting lines, add polish to the room.

Materials

- Two contrasting fabrics, according to measurements
- Contrasting fabric for piping
- Piping cord
- Hook and loop tape
- Fusible interfacing

Construction

1. Refer to page 24 for measuring, cutting, and assembly instructions, noting the following details. Face the cover top rather than hemming along the open edge to provide a seam for the insertion of the piping, then sew the piping into the seam.

2. Space small hook and loop tape "buttons" approximately 5" (13 cm) apart along the opening, then sew the loop pieces to the flap on the cover bottom, just inside the fold. Sew the corresponding hook pieces just inside the piped edge of the cover top facing.

3. Fuse a strip of interfacing to the wrong side of the facing to reinforce behind the closures.

QUILTED BEDSPREAD

Materials

- Fabric with little cross-grain stretch, according to measurements
- Fairly thin batting
- Safety pins or quilting pins
- Fabric marking pen

Measuring and Cutting

Determine the size of the finished bedspread. From that, subtract the finished width of the borders. Add 1/2" (1.3 cm) seam allowances at the outer edges of the central section. Cut the front, back, and batting to these measurements.

Add seam allowances to both the inner and outer edges of the borders. To determine the cutting length of the border strips, use the finished measurement for that side of the bedspread and extend each end by the finished width of the border plus 1/2" seam allowance. For example: If the bedspread is 90" (228 cm) along one side and the finished border will be 3" (7.5 cm) wide, border strips for that side would be cut 4" (10 cm) wide and 97" (245.6 cm) in length. Cut two strips (front and back) for each edge.

Construction

1. Layer the back, front, and batting. Pin the layers at intervals with safety or quilting pins.

2. Mark the quilting lines. Use a fabric marking pen with disappearing or washable ink, testing first on fabric scraps.

3. Stitch along the marked lines, stitching a single line of the entire pattern first and then stitching the parallel lines. Trim and square the edges.

4. On the central front and back pieces mark the point at each corner where the seamlines intersect. Mark the midpoint of each side. Mark the midpoint of each border strip.

5. Stitch a border strip to each edge of the front, with right sides together, matching the midpoints and starting and ending the stitching exactly at the marked corner points.

6. Miter all corners by folding the cover in half diagonally, wrong side out. Then align the raw edges of the border ends. Place a ruler along the diagonal fold and draw a line from the marked corner point (the end of the stitching line) to the midpoint of the border. Mark this point. Draw another line, at a precise right angle to the previous line, from the marked point of the border midpoint to the seamline at the outer edge, as shown in the illustration. Repeat for the opposite corner, then refold the cover diagonally in the other direction and mark the remaining two corners.

7. Stitch each corner, beginning exactly at the marked corner of the cover/border seam and keeping the seam allowances free. Stitch to the marked point on the inner line, then take one or two short stitches across the diagonal, then stitch to the marked point on the outer seamline of the border. Shorten the stitch length at the beginning and end of stitching lines as before.

8. Clip corners, turn, and press. On the wrong side of the cover, fold the border seam allowances under to just cover the stitching line. Press. Stitch invisibly by hand, or baste and then turn to the right side and stitch in the ditch on the border seamline.

DESIGNER NOTE

If you're lucky, you may have just enough fabric from the room's larger decorating projects to cover two plump pillows. For added pillow softness, wrap common pillow forms with inch-thick fiberfill batting. (Instructions for basic knife-edge pillows are on page 18; for piping, page 16.)

CHAPTER 2

Easy Living

Wing chairs *with* back-buttoned slipcovers

The slipcover on this wing chair, with a T-shaped deck and box cushion, features piping around the outer edges and fastens down both sides of the back with fabric-covered buttons. For beginners, a quick study of the sidebars on pages 73 and 75 may prove helpful.

Materials

- Fabric, according to measurements (heavy slubbed cotton in a solid color is a good beginner's choice)
- Piping cord, 1/4" to 3/8" (.5 to 1 cm) in diameter
- Zipper
- Button covering kit and buttons
- T-pins for fitting
- Useful but not essential: rotary cutter and mat

Measuring and Cutting

As each section is measured, give it an ID number or letter, then label it as it's cut—rectangles can look very much alike. Record the measurements.

With a chalk marker draw the intended seamlines of the cover on the chair upholstery to define each area that will be measured. For example, mark the line around the top and wings, the line where arm section will meet front, and the arm/outer wing seamline location. For the seamlines that will extend from the arms up the edges of the wings and across the back, mark the seamline on the chair toward the outside so that the outer wings and outer back pieces will be fairly flat and so that necessary fitting around the chair's curves will be done on the inner back and inner wing pieces.

For your initial cutting allow plenty of ease on each piece. Measure the widest point of each section, then add 2" to 5"(5 cm to 13 cm) to finished measurements for cutting, allowing the greater amount where fitting will be necessary on curves and corners. The pieces will be fitted on the chair and adjustments made then. For seams that won't require any fitting, such as those joining widths of the skirt, add a 1/2" (1.5 cm) seam allowance at each edge. On all pieces ending at the deck, add a tuck-in allowance of 6" (15 cm).

Be careful to cut separate left and right pieces where necessary.

A. Skirt. Tie a string around the chair at the point where the upper edge of the skirt will be, making sure it is at an even distance from the floor all around. Measure the length to the floor or as desired. Figure the number of fabric widths needed to make up the skirt, planning so that seams will be located inside the pleats. On the chair shown, the box pleats are spaced 5" (12.5 cm) apart and are 2-1/2" (6.5 cm) deep.

The main section of the skirt, surrounding the sides and front of the chair, ends in underlay at each back corner. Each underlay is 2" (5 cm) wide, with 1-3/4" (5.5 cm) added for hem. This area will not be pleated. On the smaller back skirt section it may be necessary to adjust the pleat spacing so that there is a pleat right at each edge.

With all but very heavy fabrics the skirt will hang better if it is lined with a stable lightweight fabric. Cut the skirt with 2" (5.5 cm) added to the finished length measurement. Cut the lining 1" (2.5 cm) shorter than the skirt.

With lightweight fabric the skirt length can simply be doubled to create a self-lining. Substitute seam allowance for the hem allowance at each back corner and eliminate the hem allowance at the lower edge.

With heavier fabric, use a lightweight fabric for the lining. On both the skirt and lining substitute a seam allowance for the hem allowance at the two back corners. For the skirt, add 1" to the length, and add upper and lower seam allowances. Cut lining 1" shorter, and add seam allowances.

B. Front and deck. Measure the height and depth from the skirt seamline up the front to the inner back. For width, measure around the front between the outer arm seamlines. Add 6" for tuck-in at the back. Cut one.

C. Arms. Measure the length from the skirt seamline on the outside over the arm to the deck. Add 6" for the tuck-in at the lower inside edges. Measure the width from the seamline at the front of the arm to the wing seamlines. Cut two, a left and a right.

D. Arm front. Measure the length from the upper edge of arm front to the deck. Add extra length at the lower edge. Measure the width across the widest point of the arm front. Cut two, a left and a right.

E. Inner back. For width, measure from corner to corner at the widest point. In length measure from the predetermined upper edge to the deck. Add 6" for tuck-in along the lower edge. Cut one.

F. Inner wings. For width, measure from the edge seamline across wing at widest point to the inner back seamline. Measure the length to deck, and add 6" for tuck-in. Cut two, a left and a right.

G. Outer wings. Measure the width at the widest point, from the edge seamline across the wing to about 6" beyond the back corner seamline. Measure the length from the upper seamline to the skirt seamline. Cut two, a left and a right.

H. Outer back. Measure across the widest point between the corner seamlines and add 3" (8 cm) at each side. For length, measure from the upper seamline to the skirt seamline.

I. Seat cushion. Measure for the T-style cushion as for other box cushions following the instructions on page 93. A zipper, 4" (10 cm) longer than the back width of cushion, will be installed along the welt, or boxing strip, across the back, and around both back corners.

J. Piping. Because many of the piped seams are along curves, fabric strips to cover the piping cord should be cut on the bias. Allow 4" in width for each strip. To determine the total length of piping needed, measure these seamlines: from top of the skirt up and around wing, across the back, and down the other side to the skirt; around the front of arm from the skirt seam to the deck, times two; around the skirt seam. If desired, also pipe the cushion seams around the upper and lower welt edges. To the total add 18" (46 cm) or so for waste.

Detailed instructions for making and sewing piping are on page 16.

Fitting

1. Fit the cover to the chair wrong side out, a section at a time. Take time to pin carefully and mark accurately. The fit should be smooth but not tight.

2. Secure each piece to the chair with a few pins, then pin exactly along the intended seamlines, placing the pins close together. Large T-pins work best for pinning thick layers of fabric and they are easier to find and remove when stitching.

3. Plan 1/2" (1.5 cm) seam allowances (wider with very thick fabric) and mark the cutting lines with chalk. If it's necessary to trim or clip to fit a piece, cut away the least possible amount of fabric until the fit is certain.

4. Fold tucks or darts along curved seamlines. Plan piped seams on the cover so they won't fall exactly along piped seams of the upholstery. After pinning carefully mark all seamlines with a fabric marking pen.

5. Position the front/deck piece. At the back and sides fold the edges of fabric to the center. Allow 3" for tuck-in around these sides, plus seam allowances. Even with the

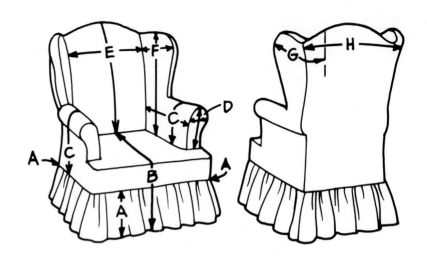

fronts of the arms, carefully clip the fabric from the edges toward the arms, making the cut just long enough that the front of the piece can wrap smoothly around the corners. Fold the lower front edges around to the marked front/arm seamlines. Pin darts at the front corners. Pin at the seamlines and chalk-mark cutting lines.

6. Inner back. Anchor this piece with pins as for the front/deck. Fit the top to outer back seamline, easing over the back curve and pinning small tucks as necessary. At the lower edge match to the deck piece, allowing the same amount for tuck-in.

7. Inner wings. Ease around the outer wing curves, match the seamlines to the inner back and tuck-in to deck.

8. Outer wings. Pin to seamlines around the wings and at arm joints. From top to bottom of the piece draw a line to mark the corner where chair wing joins back. Allow 2-1/2" (6.5 cm) in width beyond marked line for underlay and to add ease.

9. Outer back. Pin only across the top. Fold under the edges at the back/wing corner lines. Mark the cutting lines 1-3/4" (4.5 cm) outside each fold.

10. Arms. Fit to the outer wings, then the inner wings. At the inner wing's seamline, clip from the edge in toward the seamline as necessary for a smooth fit. Match the tuck-in at the deck.

11. Arm fronts. Fit to the arm, keeping the arm front piece as flat as possible and easing the fronts of the arm pieces over rounded areas. At the lower edge, match the tuck-in where this piece joins the inner arm, tapering to a flat fit where the arm front joins the outer arm and the lower front.

12. Skirt. Adjust the lower edges of all pieces at the skirt line and mark.

Construction

Carefully unpin the cover, making sure all seamlines are marked well. Assemble the pieces in the same order they were fitted on the chair, above. For curved seams, such as the arm/wing and inner/outer wing seams, or any area that caused difficulty in fitting, baste the seam first and try it over the chair right side out. Trim away excess seam allowances once fit is satisfactory.

1. Make the piping according to the instructions on page 16. Sew piping to the outer edge of each arm section, on the right side, stitching exactly on the marked seamline.

2. Stitch darts in front/deck section. Sew the piping to the right side of the arm pieces around the front edges. Align the piping seamline with the arm seamline.

3. Sew the front/deck to the inner arms, then sew arm fronts to arms.

4. Join the ends of the deck section to the lower edges of the arm fronts and to the lower edges of the outer arms. Reinforce the seam where a clip was made to fit the corner by stitching again in the seam allowance 1/8" (2 mm) from previous stitching.

5. Stitch the inner wings to the inner back. Sew the inner wings to the arms; sew the inner wings and back to the deck.

6. For each outer wing, cut a strip of fusible interfacing 2" (5 cm) wide and the length of the underlay edge. Fuse interfacing to wrong side of the underlays between the hemline and the lap line for the outer back section. Fold under the underlay hems; stitch.

7. On the outer back, fold under the side hems 1-3/4" (4.5 cm); press. Fold under the raw edge 1/2" (1.5 cm); press. Fuse a strip of interfacing to each side between the folds of the hems. Stitch along the outermost fold on each side.

8. Work buttonholes along the outer edges of the back. Refer to the photo as a spacing guide.

9. Baste the outer back to the outer wings along the upper edge, matching the finished back edges to the marked lines on the wings.

10. Stitch piping to the right side of the back/outer wings around the outer edge of the piece, placing the piping stitching line on the marked seamline of the cover piece.

11. Sew the outer wings and back to the inner wings and back, and to the arms. Hem the lower edges of both skirt pieces. Hem the ends to correspond to the ends of the back wing underlays and the outer back edges. If a lining will be used, stitch the lower edges of the skirt and the lining with right sides together. Align the upper raw edges and stitch the ends. Turn right side out and baste the skirt and lining together across the upper edge. Pleat the larger skirt section. Match hemmed ends to underlays and make half a pleat at each marked back corner. Space so there is a pleat at each front corner. Pleat the back skirt section in the same way, with half a pleat at each back corner.

13. Baste the pleats in place, stitching on both sides of the seamline. Stitch piping to the right side of the skirt, matching seamlines. Place the cover on the chair and mark the button positions.

14. Make the seat cushion cover according to the instructions on page 93.

SELECTING AND BUYING FABRIC

An ideal slipcover fabric is heavy enough and sturdy enough to withstand hard use, but not so heavy that a home sewing machine cannot sew through six or eight layers of it. Choose a firmly woven fabric with little or no stretch, such as medium- to heavy-weight linen, cotton, or blends. Textured fabrics such as tweeds work well. Avoid slippery fabrics, and avoid upholstery fabrics coated on the wrong side—they can be very difficult to sew with a home machine. A novice should pass up wide stripes, plaids, or other patterns that require matching. Heavy, slubbed cotton is a good choice for beginners because it eliminates worries about matching or positioning patterns, and the surface texture also helps disguise less-than-perfect stitching and fitting.

After measurements have been taken, make a diagram on graph paper to calculate fabric yardage. All pieces that will be vertical on the chair should be cut on lengthwise grain of fabric, the direction with the least stretch. The depth of the seat cushion—front to back—also is best cut on the lengthwise grain. The completed diagram can be used to calculate yardage.

The amount of fabric needed will depend upon size of the chair, fabric width, and whether matching is required. For a high-backed wing chair, plan to buy approximately 10 to 12 yards (9 to 11 m). Always buy an extra yard or two just to be safe. Extra fabric is always useful for arm covers, an extra seat cushion cover, throw pillows, or small decorative accessories. Buy all yardage from the same bolt; there can be minor color differences that become obvious once a project is complete.

Slipcover *and* floral footstool

Heavy cotton fabric in a random floral print is an excellent fabric choice for slipcovers. The cotton is comfortable, easy to care for, and one of the best fabrics to work with, and the floral print requires no matching.

Materials
FOR SLIPCOVER AND FOOTSTOOL

• Fabric, according to measurements

Construction
FOR SLIPCOVER AND FOOTSTOOL

The slipcover can be made following the instructions for the wingback chair on page 70 with the following changes.

1. Since this slipcover has no skirt, the front, arms, arm fronts, outer wings, and back are measured to the floor. Add a 2" (5 cm) hem allowance for a finished double hem of 1-1/2" (4 cm).

2. Ties, instead of buttons and buttonholes, fasten the cover at the outer back corners. On the outer back, stitch tie securely to the hem, then stitch the hem through all thicknesses. Stitch corresponding ties to the outer wing sections.

3. Complete instructions for the footstool are on page 124.

GETTING READY TO SEW

Prepare the fabric before cutting. One advantage of slipcovers is that they can be removed for laundering or dry cleaning. If the cover will be washed, the fabric must be washed and dried before it is cut (see page 10). After measurements are taken and approximate sizes of pieces are figured, the fabric can be cut into sections for easier washing and drying. Straighten the grainlines (see page 10) to ensure the cover will hang correctly.

A large project like this one will be easier to handle if there is adequate table space for cutting, sewing, and pressing. A large cutting mat and rotary cutter will greatly speed the cutting-out steps. For pressing, use a table with a top that won't be damaged by steam. Cover it with a thick layer of newspaper, then with several layers of old wool (not synthetic) blankets.

Have the sewing machine in good working order: oiled, clean and free of lint, with tension and feed dogs in adjustment. For heavy fabric use size 90/14 to 110/18 "jeans" needles, which have sharp points instead of the slightly rounded "universal" point found on most needles. Keep some spares on hand; it may be necessary to replace the needle once or twice during the project. Sew with the machine on a large table to support the weight of the fabric to avoid placing a strain on the feed dogs or breaking a needle.

Checked room

This room blends oranges, blues, and ivories for an inviting warmth. The tailored table cover is a great project choice to recycle an old table or even a wooden crate. The fabric-covered box and multi-technique pillows allow you to play with additional prints and blends.

Materials

- An old table or wooden box
- 1" thick foam to fit top
- Fabric, according to measurements
- Piping or piping cord
- Strips of adhesive-backed hook and loop tape

Measuring and Cutting

Use hook and loop tape to secure the foam pad to the table top. With the foam in place, measure the length, width, and height of the table. Allow 1/2" (1.5 cm) for each seam allowance. For the top, add 1" (3 cm) to the height and width measurements for seam allowances; cut one piece.

The finished length of the welt equals twice the width plus twice the length measurements, plus seam allowances. Plan so that the seams will be at the corners, and add seam allowances as necessary. The width of the welt will depend upon the height of the table and the designer's eye. Be sure, though, that the finished welt width and finished skirt length add up to the table's height measurement. Add seam allowances on the upper and lower sides of the welt.

For the skirt, locate the necessary seams at the corners. To the finished length and width measurements add 4" (10 cm) at each side of each piece to make a 2" (5 cm) box pleat at each corner.

Add seam allowance at the upper edge and 1-1/2" (3.5 cm) for a double hem at the lower edge. If you're making your own piping, cut bias strips long enough to reach twice around the table.

Construction

1. Make the corded piping (page 16) and stitch around the top on the right side. Join the ends of the welt pieces in a continuous loop. Stitch the piping along the seamline at the lower edge.

2. Stitch the skirt together at the sides. Baste the corner pleats in place. With right sides together, stitch the skirt to the welt, stitching on the welt piping stitching line.

3. With right sides together, stitch the welt/skirt to the top, stitching on top of the piping stitching line.

COUCH PILLOWS

Materials

- Fabric
- Pillow form or stuffing
- Piping or piping cord

Construction

1. Make the piping from bias cut fabric, referring to page 16 if needed. (Purchased piping may be substituted.)

2. Refer to the basic knife-edge pillow instructions on page 18 for cutting and assembly directions.

Daybed pillows

Pillows covered with fabric left over from draperies and slipcovers soften room's lines and pull the elements together. Several varieties of pillows were created from just two simple styles, and contrasting piping and varied fabric backs add visual appeal.

Materials

- Contrasting fabrics
- Pillow forms or stuffing
- Zippers (optional)
- Piping (optional)

Construction

Refer to the basic knife-edge and bolster pillow instructions on pages 18 and 22. Add visual interest by using contrasting piping and different front and back fabrics.

Pillows, pillows, pillows

This is a real change-the-decor-in-a-day project. The pillows shown here are the quickest and easiest styles to make. With a rotary cutter and mat, fabrics for each cover size can be stacked and cut all at once.

SQUARE PILLOWS

Materials

- Fabric
- Purchased pillow form or stuffing
- Rotary cutter and mat (optional)

Construction

Refer to the basic cutting and assembly instructions for knife-edge pillows on page 18.

ROUND PILLOWS

Materials

- Fabric
- Foam, 1" thick, according to desired finished pillow size
- 1/2" (1.5 cm) batting
- Ribbon

Construction

Make a form by tightly rolling a piece of foam and then wrapping with batting. Cut out a tube shape of fabric with the ends slightly extended and stitch the cover according to the instructions for the duffel pillow with extended ends are on page 22.

Seat cushions

As beautiful as antique chairs are, they can sometimes be a little uncomfortable for long-term seating. These soft seat cushions are reversible — a patterned cotton fabric on one side and a solid color on the other. Extra-long ties at the corners are made with a piece of each fabric.

Materials

- Fabric, according to measurements
- Purchased cushions

Construction

1. Refer to the basic instructions for knife-edge pillows on page 18 for measuring and cutting fabric. Cut the back corners on the diagonal to accommodate the chair posts.

2. Make four ties for each cushion with a finished size of 1" (2.5 cm) wide by 24" (60 cm) long. (See page 13 for complete instructions for making ties.)

3. Pin two ties into the seam on the back and the side of the cushion, on either side of the diagonal corner.

4. Finish assembling the cushions as directed on page 93.

Pillow play

The simplest pillow construction is used here in a most imaginative way! Two knife-edge pillows are tied and buttoned to a third pillow to create a pillow "sandwich." The outer pillows are filled with fiberfill batting, the inner one utilizes a purchased pillow form.

GREEN PLAID TIED PILLOW

Materials

- Two compatible fabrics
- Fiberfill batting, 1" (2.5 cm) thick
- Pillow form, 2" (5 cm) thick
- Button covering kit and 2 large buttons

Construction

1. Refer to the basic knife-edge pillow instructions beginning on page 18. Make 16 15-inch (38 cm) long ties.

2. Cut out squares for three pillows, using the size of your pillow form as a guide. Pin the ties into the seams of the two batting pillows at each corner and the midpoint on each side.

3. Finish assembling the pillows, then fill two of them with batting and the third with the pillow form. Cover the two buttons with fabric scraps according to the manufacturer's instructions.

4. Place the pillow form pillow between the batting pillows and tie the ties. Sew the fabric-covered buttons to each other through all of the thicknesses.

RED STRIPED PILLOW

Materials

- Fabric, according to measurements
- Piping cording
- Button covering kit and 2 buttons

Construction

1. Cut the fabric, referring to the basic instructions for bolster pillows beginning on page 22. Make the piping and sew it into the seam at the ends of the roll, then finish assembling the pillow.

2. Cover the button according to the manufacturer's instructions, then sew them in place at the center of each end to cover the raw edges.

Coral
dining room

Made from a heavy, linen-weave cotton, the
chair covers derive their precise fit from a narrow gusset sewn between the inner and outer
back sections. A box pleat at each front corner eases the fit around the lower part of the
chair and softens the cover's tailored lines.

- Fabric, according to measurements
- Piping cord, approximately 1/4" (7 mm) diameter, according to measurements

Measuring and Cutting

Add 1/2" (1.5 cm) to measurements wherever seam allowance is required. Add 1-1/2" (4 cm) at the lower edges for a 3/4" (2 cm) finished double hem.

Measure the width and depth of the seat. Add seam allowance to all sides and cut one. Mark the seamline intersections at the corners.

Measure the inner back, from the seat to the center point at the top back. Measure the width and add seam allowances to all sides, then cut one.

Measure the outer back from the center point at the top back to the floor (or desired length). Measure the width. Add seam allowances to the top and sides and add a hem allowance at the lower edge. Cut one.

For the gusset, measure the width of the back posts just above the seat, at the top, and halfway between. Cut a newspaper pattern for this piece to check the fit. Add seam allowances on all sides, and cut one left and one right.

For the skirt, measure from the back corner, just below the top of the seat, to the front corner. Measure the front between the corners. At the front corners add 6" (15 cm) to the side and front measurements for pleats. The total finished skirt width should be twice the side measurement plus the front measurement plus 24" (60 cm). If it will be necessary to piece the fabric to obtain the necessary skirt width, be sure to place the piecing seam in a pleat and remember to add seam allowances for this seam. Measure the skirt length from the top of the seat to the floor, or the desired point, as for the outer back. Add seam allowance at the sides and the upper edge, and a hem allowance at the lower edge.

Use the seat measurements to determine the piping length.

Construction

1. Make the piping, referring to the detailed piping instructions on page 16 if necessary. Sew to the right side of the seat, matching seamlines and tapering ends into seams at the back corners. Sew the seat to the inner back, beginning and ending the stitching at the side seamlines of the seat. Sew the inner back to the outer back across the top.

2. Sew the gussets between the inner and outer back, beginning and ending the stitching at the seamline on the gusset's lower edge.

3. Stitch the piecing seams in the skirt, if necessary. Fold the pleats at the front corners. Pin, then test-fit on the chair. On the wrong side, stitch closed the upper 3" (8 cm) of each pleat. Stitch the skirt to the seat, gusset, and outer back. Hem the lower edge.

Pink stripes *and* roses dining room

This cheerful dining area becomes a comfortable guest room when needed. When you're shopping for fabrics, remember how well the bold pink striped chintz in these projects works with the delicate rose print.

FUTON COVER

Materials

- Fabric, according to measurements
- Zipper

Measuring and Cutting

Measure across the width of the cushion top/bottom from the exact midpoint on one edge to the midpoint on the opposite edge. If the cushion is rectangular rather than square, also measure the length in the same way. Add a seam allowance on all four sides and cut two pieces the same size.

Construction

1. Stitch the pieces with right sides together, installing a centered zipper in one of the seams. For this cover style use a zipper approximately 4" (10 cm) shorter than the seam.

2. Slip the cover over the cushion and tuck in the corners.

PILLOWS

Materials

- Fabric
- Zippers
- Pillow form or stuffing
- Piping (optional)

Construction

1. Refer to the basic cutting and assembling instructions on page 18. The smaller pink striped pillows are made with the knife-edge technique. They have zippers on the back, and they are trimmed with solid pink piping

2. The ruffled pillows are also made with the knife-edge technique, but with sham openings across the backs. The floral print pillows have ruffles made of doubled fabric. On the smaller one, pink piping is incorporated into the seam. The large white sham has a hemmed single-thickness ruffle. Complete instructions for making ruffles are on page 000

Short dining chair covers

If you tend to bore easily with your decor, then this is the project for you. Make each chair cover in the same style, but choose a different contrasting fabric for each chair to liven things up.

Materials

- Fabric, according to measurements

Measuring and Cutting

Cut the back, pleat, and underlay as one piece, fabric width permitting. If piecing is necessary, plan so that the piecing seam will be at the inner fold of the pleat if possible. To cut the back, make the initial pattern as described on page 31. Mark a center back point on the second piece of newspaper. Mark a point 6" (15 cm) on each side of center. Fold the two outer marks to meet at the center and continue the folds evenly down the length of the paper. Use the original pattern to shape the upper edge and for length and width. Add seam and hem allowances. Cut the pattern and unfold it. Cut in half down the center back line and place this line on folded fabric to cut the fabric.

A newspaper pattern should also be made for a rounded seat like this one. The seamline at the seat back should match the lower seamline of the inner back. To check measurements, make sure that along the side seamline the length of the inner back and skirt, excluding seam allowances, equals that of the outer back.

The ties are 24" (60 cm) long and 1" (2.5 cm) wide and are finished at both ends. Each tie end is positioned 1-1/2" from the center back fold of the pleat, then stitched in place with an X through both thicknesses of fabric.

Construction

This cover is made according to the instructions on page 31, with a few changes. A single fabric is used for the entire cover, the skirt is shorter, and smaller ties are sewn to the back pleat.

Plaid cushions

A narrow fabric skirt, curved slightly along the front, trims the front and sides of these chair cushions, serving the double purpose of hiding chair edges and preventing splinters from shredding stockings.

Materials

- Fabric, according to measurements

Measuring and Cutting

Make a pattern on kraft paper or newspaper. Measure the sides, front, and back of the chair seat and draw this shape. Add 1/2" (1.5 cm) seam allowances all around and use this pattern for the bottom of the cushion.

Draw around the pattern on another sheet of paper to make the pattern for the cushion top. Extend the sides 3/4" (2 cm) at the front. Extend the front by 3/4" on each side. Extend the original side and front lines to the new lines and mark that point on each side of both corners. Draw a diagonal line from each new front corner through the original front corner to a length of 2-1/2" (6.5 cm). Draw a line from the inner end of this line to each of the marked points adjacent to the corner. These will be stitching lines for the darts. Add seam allowances and extend the dart stitching lines to the cutting lines.

The skirt is a double layer of fabric with a seam along the lower edge, sewn into the edge seam of the cushion. It extends along the sides and front of the cushion only.

Cut a paper pattern. For width, use the chair seat depth and the front width measurements and add 2" (5 cm) at each side of each front corner for box pleats. Cut the piece 2" in height.

Fold the pattern in half to mark center front of the chair. Fold pleats in place at the corners. To cut from fabric, taper the length of the skirt to 3" (7.5 cm) or as desired at the center front. Add seam allowances at all edges; cut two.

Cut four strips for the ties, each 14" (36 cm) long and 2" wide. Measurements include 1/4" (.5 cm) seam allowances; finished ties will be 3/4" (2 cm) wide.

Construction

Make the cushion according to the instructions for the knife-edge pillow cover, page 18, noting the following differences.

1. Using the pattern pieces for the cover top and bottom, make a liner and fill it. Stitch darts in the top cover section.

2. Stitch the skirt sections, right sides together, along the lower edge and ends. Trim, turn, and press. Fold and baste the front corner pleats. Fold in seam allowances on the long edges and one end of the ties. Stitch along both edges and across the end.

3. Place the cover bottom piece right side up on a table. Place the skirt on it, outer side up with raw edges and corners aligned. Place the ties adjacent to the back corners, raw edges aligned with cover and skirt edges. Now add the cover top, wrong side up. Pin and stitch all layers, leaving an opening for turning if needed.

Striped chair covers

These chair covers allow you to play with contempoary stripes and other trendy prints without making the enormous investment of new furniture.

Materials

- Fabric, according to measurements

Measuring and Cutting

Make a diagram for each piece of the cover and write in the measurements. Use the drawings to plan a cutting layout and calculate yardage requirements. Add 1/2" (1.5 cm) seam allowance where required. For the skirt and back add 1-1/2" (3.5 cm) for a 1" (2.5 cm) finished double hem.

The seat and inner back will be cut as a single piece. Measure the depth of the chair seat from the front to the back, then up the inner back to the top. Measure the width across the inner back, across seat back, and across the seat front. Add seam allowances on all sides, and cut from fabric. On the fabric, mark the point at each side where seat joins back.

Determine the skirt length by measuring from the seat top to the desired length. For the width of the skirt use the seat depth and width as measured in paragraph 1. If it will be necessary to piece the skirt, plan so that the seam will be inside a pleat. At each side of each front corner add 4" (10 cm) for a pleat. Add seam allowance at the sides and upper edge; add hem allowance at the lower edge.

Measure the outer back across the top. Measure across again at the lower edge of the seat, beginning and ending at the point where the measurement for the seat/inner back width was taken. Cut a newspaper pattern to these measurements.

Fold the pattern in half lengthwise, then in half again to mark the upper back into quarters. Make another pattern for the back pleat and underlay. From another sheet of newspaper cut a strip 9" (23 cm) wide and somewhat longer than the chair back pattern. Fold the outer edges of the piece 1/2" (1.5 cm) toward the center. Now bring the folded edges together to meet at the center, so that

each side is 2" (5 cm) wide. Open up the folds of the large back pattern piece and place it over this one, with the center folds directly under one of the outer foldlines of the back pattern. Draw the line of the upper back onto the new pattern piece. Draw another line 1/2" outside this one for the cutting line. At the lower edge add the hem allowance and draw the cutting line.

When cutting these pieces from fabric, cut from doubled fabric or cut one with the pattern piece right side up and one with it upside down.

Cut the back pattern along the outer foldlines. Use one of the smaller pieces for the outer sides. Add seam and hem allowances, and cut a right and a left side. Add seam and hem allowances to the center back piece, and cut one from fabric.

Cut 12 strips of fabric for ties, each 13" (33 cm) long and 2-1/2" (6.5 cm) wide.

Construction

1. Make the ties. On each strip fold one end 1/2" (1 cm) to the wrong side; press. Fold the strip in half lengthwise, right side out; press. Fold both long edges in toward the first fold; press. Stitch close to both long edges and across the finished end.

2. Assemble the back. Position three ties on the right side of each side back section with the unfinished ends aligning with the inner edge of the piece. Pin the ties in corresponding positions on both sides of the center back section. Baste. With right sides together, pin the pleat/underlay pieces to the side back and the center back pieces. Stitch, keeping the ties free. Press the seams open.

3. On the outside, fold and press along the seamlines to form the pleats. Bring the seams together, making both pleats equal in width. Baste across the top.

4. Stitch the skirt sections together if necessary. Fold the box pleat at each front corner. Mark a point 4" (10 cm) to each side of the corner point and bring the marks together at the corner. Baste across the upper edge.

5. On the seat/back piece staystitch the front corners and across the marked points at the seat back. Clip through the seam allowance almost to the marks.

6. Stitch the skirt to the seat/back piece, matching the front corners and matching the seamlines at the skirt back to the marked points at the back of the seat.

7. Stitch the back to the inner back and skirt. Hem the lower edge all around, then topstitch along the outer folds of the back pleats.

Teatime ambiance

A family of cotton print fabrics is artfully combined to provide cheery ambiance for teatime. The napkins feature wonderful detailing such as the teapot appliqué, a reversible mitered border, and narrow, uncorded piping in the border seam. The tablecloth can be made from scratch or a purchased cloth can be embellished with borders and appliqués. The chair seats and backs were made from a coordinating fabric, and were reinforced with sew-in interfacing.

Materials
FOR EACH NAPKIN

- Solid color cotton or linen fabric for central part of napkin
- Solid color or complementary print cotton or linen fabric for piping, if used, and for borders (A fabric with no discernable right or wrong side will work best.)
- Motif cut from print fabric for appliqué
- Paper-backed fusible web for appliqué
- Helpful but not essential: a clear plastic ruler with bias markings

Measuring and Cutting

Determine the finished size of the napkin. Directions are for a napkin 12" (31 cm) square, a good size for luncheon or tea. An 18" to 20" (45 to 50 cm) square makes a generously sized dinner napkin. The border is 1" (3 cm) wide all around. Seam allowances are 1/2" (1.5 cm).

Cut a 11" (28 cm) square for the central part of the napkin.

Cut four strips for the borders, 13" (34 cm) long and 3" (6 cm) wide. To make the napkin a different size, cut border strips to the finished napkin length plus double the seam allowance.

For piping, cut a bias strip 41" (103 cm) long and 1-1/4" (3.5 cm) wide. (Complete instructions for making piping and piecing bias strips are on page 16.)

Construction

1. Fold the piping strip in half lengthwise, right side out, and press lightly. On the seamline, mark a point 1/2" (1.5 cm) from each end. Fold in half, matching the marked points, and mark the halfway point on the seamline. Fold again and mark two points, so the strip is divided into quarters with seam allowances at each end. Staystitch along the seamline below each marked point for about an inch (2.5 cm), using a fairly short stitch length.

2. Mark the seamline intersection at each corner on the right side of the square. Position the piping on the square, matching the marked points and taking care that the raw edges are aligned. At the corners clip the piping seam allowances diagonally to the staystitching. Overlap the ends at the beginning/ending corner. Stitch.

3. Mark the inner corner positions on the right side seamline of each border strip, 1-1/2" (4.5 cm) from each end. Pin the border strips to the square with right sides together, matching corners. Sew, stitching on piping stitching line, beginning and ending stitching exactly at corners. Use a very short stitch length at the beginning and ending of seams. Press the seam allowances toward border.

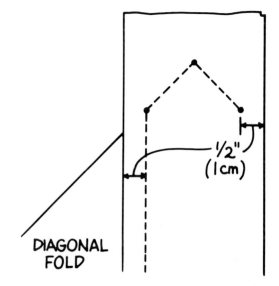

DIAGONAL FOLD

½" (1cm)

4. Miter the corners. Fold the napkin in half diagonally, wrong side out. Align the raw edges of the border ends. At each corner draw a straight line 1" (3 cm) from the stitching line and parallel to it, extending from the napkin/border corner toward the border ends. Draw another line parallel to the first and 1" from it. This is the outer seamline. Draw a line exactly perpendicular to these two lines from the sewn corner to the outer border seamline. Mark this point on the outer seamline. Place a ruler along the diagonal fold of the napkin and across the border. Draw a line extending the diagonal foldline onto the border, stopping at the first inner line. Mark this point.Repeat for the opposite corner, then refold the napkin diagonally in the other direction and mark the remaining two corners.

5. Stitch each corner, beginning exactly at the marked corner of the napkin/border seam and keeping the seam allowances free. Stitch to the marked point on the inner line, then take one short stitch across the diagonal and then stitch to the marked point on the outer seamline of the border. Shorten the stitch length at the beginning and end of stitching lines as before. Clip corners, turn, and press.

6. On the napkin's wrong side fold the border seam allowances under to just cover the stitching line. Press. Stitch invisibly by hand, or baste and turn to the right side and stitch exactly on the piping/border seamline.

7. Press bonding web to the appliqué's wrong side, referring to the manufacturer's directions. Trim carefully around the motif, remove the paper backing, and press in place on the napkin. Stitch around the motif with a fairly open zigzag stitch set at medium width.

Materials and equipment

- Solid color fabric or purchased tablecloth
- Print fabric for border and appliqués
- Paper-backed fusible web
- Handy but not essential: rotary cutter, cutting mat, ruler, bias tape maker

Measuring and Cutting

For a custom tablecloth, cut the fabric to the desired dimensions. Cut bias strips to make up the necessary length, plus about 4" (10 cm) extra. This job is fast and easy with a rotary cutter and mat. If a bias tape maker will be used, cut strips to the width indicated for a finished tape width of 5/8" to 3/4" (1.5 to 2 cm), or as desired. Without a tape maker, cut strips 1" (3 cm) wider than the desired finished border width. Piece strips as described on page 16.

Construction

1. Hem the tablecloth edges with a narrow double hem, mitering the corners (see page 19).

2. Fold the tape through the tape maker and press, or fold the raw edges 1/2" (1.5 cm) to the wrong side and press, taking care not to stretch the fabric.

3. Starting on a straight edge rather than at a corner, pin the border in place. At the corners, crease tape on wrong side to miter; press.

4. Stitch the border to the cloth along both edges, using a straight stitch or a narrow, open zigzag stitch. Appliqué the motifs wherever desired, according to step 7 for the bordered napkin.

Materials

- Sturdy fabric with little or no stretch, according to measurements
- Interfacing, if needed, according to measurements

Measuring and Cutting

Remove the existing seat and back fabric to determine the measurements of the new pieces. Make note of the way seat fabric is attached to frame. Allow 1/2" (1.5 cm) for the seams and 1" (2.5 cm) for crossgrain hems (slightly more for very thick fabric). If the pieces have stretched, refit them to determine cutting measurements for new pieces. Don't add ease; almost all fabric will stretch slightly with use.

To make the back of the doubled fabric either cut the piece twice as long, or cut two pieces. Add seam allowance at the upper and lower edges. If needed, cut interfacing to the length of the finished back plus seam and hem allowances. If interfacing will be used under the seat, cut to the same size as the seat fabric.

Construction

1. To interface the back, baste interfacing to the wrong side of one back section if two will be used, or along upper or lower edge if the back is of doubled fabric.

2. For back of double fabric, stitch back section(s) with right sides together along one or both long edges to form a tube. Turn right side out, press, and topstitch with two rows of stitching along the upper and lower edges.

3. For a back of single thickness fabric, press double hems across the upper and lower edges. Stitch each with two rows of stitching. Fit tightly around the chair posts, wrapping around from front to back, and pin the ends to mark the overlap points. Stitch each end with two rows of stitching, backstitching securely at the beginning and end of seam.

4. To interface the seat, position the interfacing on the wrong side of the seat fabric and hem the two pieces together as for the back, above. Attach the seat to the frame, pulling the fabric taut.

Directors' dining room

This inviting table awaits the arrival of brunch guests. The silverware rolls, which unfold into dinner napkins, can be color-coded to each guest's chair. Note that the assorted plaid and check patterns in the napkins and director's chairs were woven into the fabric (instead of printed onto it), so the fabrics look the same on both sides.

Materials

FOR EACH SILVERWARE ROLL

- Outer fabric piece, 16-1/2" (42 cm) square
- Inner fabric piece, 15-3/4" (40 cm) wide and 5-3/4" (15 cm) long
- Ribbon, approximately 1" (2.5 cm) wide and 20" (50 cm) long
- Liquid fray retardant

Construction

1. Hem one long edge of the inner piece, folding 3/4" (2 cm) to the wrong side, pressing, and then folding the raw edge to the first fold line. Press, and stitch close to the inner fold.

2. Position the inner piece on the outer piece, wrong sides together, with the raw edges of the inner piece exactly 3/8" (1 cm) inside edges of the outer piece.

3. Press 3/4" double hems on the outer piece, covering the raw edges of the inner piece. Miter the corners, as described on page 19. Stitch hem close to the inner fold.

4. Mark vertical lines on the inner piece to define a pocket for each eating utensil. Stitch along the lines through both fabrics. Finish the cut ends of the ribbon with liquid fray retardant.

PLACE MATS

Materials

FOR EACH MAT

- Two pieces of fabric in complementary patterns, both cut 15" (39 cm) wide and 12" (28 cm) long

Construction

1. Place the fabrics right sides together and stitch around the sides with a 1/2" (1.5 cm) seam allowance, leaving a 2-1/2" (6.5 cm) opening for turning. Trim the corners, turn, and press.

2. Turn under and press seam allowances along the opening, then stitch. Topstitch around the mat, stitching approximately 1/4" (7 mm) from the edge.

3. If desired, stitch a design to hold the layers together. For example, stitch a diamond pattern by sewing from the center of one side to the center of the adjacent side, continuing around the mat.

DIRECTORS' CHAIRS

Materials

- Heavy fabric, according to measurements
- Heavy interfacing (needed only if a medium-weight fabric is chosen)

Construction

Refer to page 99 for measuring and assembly instructions.

Balloon curtains kitchen

The beauty of mellowed old woods is enhanced by the softness of balloon curtains. These are much simpler to make than they appear! Their success results from the use of a soft, sheer, airy fabric that drapes well and filters the light.

Materials

- Fabric, according to measurements
- Strip of firm interfacing, fusible or sew-in
- Ring tape, according to measurements
- Cord, according to measurements
- Mounting board: 1" x 2" (2.5 cm x 5 cm) cut to fit window frame
- Angle brackets to support board
- Screw eyes, according to measurements
- One awning cleat for each curtain
- Staple gun

Measuring and Cutting

Cut the board to fit closely inside the upper window frame. Paint or finish the board as desired. Attach support brackets to hold the board almost at the top of the window frame, with either a 1" side or 2" side up, depending on the depth of the window frame. Put the board in place temporarily for measuring.

Measure the length and width of the window inside the frame. The finished width of the curtain should be approximately 1-1/2 times the width measurements. Add 1-1/2" (4 cm) at each side for 1" (3 cm) double hems.

For the length, measure from the top rear edge of the mounting board to the bottom of window, inside the frame. Allow approximately twice this length for vertical shirring. At the top add 1" for a single hem and add the depth of the board. At the bottom add 1-1/2" for a double hem.

If it is necessary to piece the fabric widths to obtain the desired curtain width, plan for a full width to be used at the center of the panel and partial widths at one or both sides. Add seam allowances for vertical seam(s) when figuring the width. Use a French seam (page 12) to join the widths.

Determine the horizontal distance between the strips of ring tape. With the rings closer together the curtain will seem more formal, like an Austrian shade. If they are farther apart, the curtain will have a looser, more casual appearance. A tape strip will be sewed along each side hem of the curtain; others are spaced evenly across the panel. When purchasing the ring tape, allow a little extra; the rings must line up horizontally across the curtain.

One screw eye will be used for each vertical row of ring tape. It should be large enough in diameter to hold as many pieces of cord as there are vertical rows of ring tape.

Construction

1. Turn a hem on the curtain sides 1-1/2" to the wrong side; press. Turn under raw edge 1/2" (1 cm); press. Don't stitch yet. Press and stitch the single hem at the top. To hem the lower edge, fold 1-1/2" to the wrong side; press. Fold under the raw edge 1/2" (1 cm); press, and stitch close to the inner fold.

2. Along the upper hemline mark positions of the ring tape strips. Place the strips at the outer edges, straddling the inner folds of the hems. The remaining strips should be spaced evenly across the panel. Gather the top of the curtain (see page 14). Work the gathering just below the hemmed edge, and where the upper front edge of the mounting board will be. Gather to the finished length along the ring tape placement lines.

3. Draw up the gathers to the width of mounting board/inner frame measurement. Smooth out the gathering at the ring tape placement points. Behind the upper gathering line, fuse or stitch a strip of interfacing to reinforce area to be stapled.

4. Position the ring tape. The rings must line up horizontally across the panel. The lowest rings should be on the hem, about 1/2" above the lower edge. Cut the tape to extend about 1/2" beyond the top and bottom of the curtain. Press under the ends just inside the curtain edges.

5. Stitch each ring tape strip to the curtain, stitching close to both edges. The uppermost rings to be used will be about 4" (10 cm) from the curtain top. Clip off the rings above this point.

6. Staple the curtain to the top mounting board. The hemmed edge should be at the back of the board top with the lower gathering line at the front of the board's top. Staple the ends first, then the center. Staple again halfway between each pair of staples, then again halfway between these pairs. Continue this way until the fabric is held securely.

7. Place a screw eye in the underside of the mounting board above each tape strip, approximately 1/2" from the front of the board.

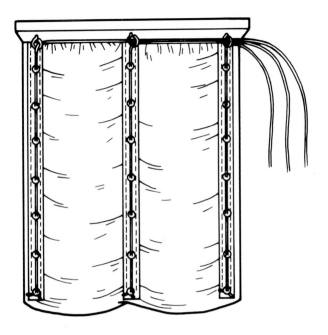

8. Rig the curtain by placing it upside down on a table or the floor. Determine the side from which the curtain will be drawn, and begin at the opposite side. Tie one end of a cord securely to the lowest ring on the tape strip, thread it up through the remaining rings, through the screw eye above the strip, then through remaining eyes on the board across to the other side. For now, leave all the cord ends long—as much as 2 ft. (60 cm) below the bottom of the curtain. Repeat for the next tape strip, threading it through all screw eyes except the first one. Continue with the remaining strips.

9. Replace the mounting board and curtain over the window. Decide where the awning cleat should be placed and attach it to the outer window trim. Braid or twist the cords, knot the ends together, and trim off any excess. Raise the curtain to the desired height and wind the cord around the cleat.

Living room comfort

A chair cover and coverlet provide a great excuse to play with plaids, and the clever piecing makes the project fun to assemble. A middle layer of warm, cotton flannel provides welcome warmth during chilly weather.

PLAID CHAIR COVER

Materials

- Fabric, according to measurements
- Piping

Measuring and Cutting

Review the cover instructions on page 87. Like that one, this slipcover has tied openings at both sides of the outer back and there is no skirt. The cover in this photo is shorter, but can be made to any desired length. Note that the seat cushion on this chair is not covered separately, but instead the front/deck piece is measured with the cushion in place and is fitted over and around it.

Cut the inner back around the marked back corners so the extensions form the upper parts of the back underlays. The lower underlays are extensions of the arm pieces.

Construction

Make the slipcover according to the detailed instructions on page 87, taking note of the following changes.

1. Fold the tucks in to fit the corners at the upper back.

2. Sew the ties into the arm front seams and knot them at the outer front corners to help the cover fit snugly. Sew the longer tie sections into the arm front/cover front seam, and sew the shorter sections into the arm front/arm seam.

3. Add piping only around the front seams.

COVERLET

Materials

- 1-7/8 yds (1.7 m) each of two complementary fabrics, 54" (137 cm) wide, for the front and back center panels
- 2-1/2 yds (2.4 m) each of two complementary fabrics for borders
- Cotton flannel, enough to make interlining piece 73" x 85" (196 cm x 231 cm)

Measuring and Cutting

The finished cover measures 72" x 84" (193 cm x 228 cm). It is made using fabric 54" wide. For fabric of different widths, piece or cut to dimensions given, or adjust the length of the upper and lower borders.

After preshrinking the fabrics, piece the cotton flannel, if necessary, to the size above. Trim away any selvages from the center panel sections so that the pieces measure 53" (129 cm) across. Trim the length to 65" (165 cm), following the crosswise grainline exactly.

Mark off the border strips on the lengthwise grain of the fabric. Plan so that the inner (and outer) edges of each are on the same stripe of the pattern so that they will match up at the mitered corners as in the photograph. Cut all strips 11" (28.5 cm) wide. From each fabric cut two strips 85" long and two strips 73" long.

Construction

1. On both center panel sections mark the seamline intersections at all four corners. Mark the center of each side. On the border strips, mark the centers of each long edge.

2. Pin a border strip to each edge of the center panel, beginning at matched centers. Stitch, beginning and ending the stitching exactly at the marked corner points. Press seam allowances toward borders.

3. Miter the corners, folding the cover diagonally with its wrong side out across corner and aligning the border seams. Mark the seamline intersection point at the outer edge of the border. Pin the ends of the border strips together at each corner, matching the marked points at outer edges. Stitch diagonally from inner to outer marked points. Press seams open.

4. Position the cover top and bottom with right sides together and align the flannel on top. Stitch, matching the marked points at the border corners. Leave an opening on one edge for turning.

Note: It is important with this design to sew exactly along stripes in the fabric. An even-feed presser foot, or walking foot, is a great boon for keeping fabric layers evenly together on long seams.

CUSHIONS AND PILLOWS

Materials

- Leftover fabric pieces from larger decorating projects
- Cushion and/or pillow forms or stuffing
- Zipper (for cushion)
- Optional piping

Construction

For the cushion, refer to the instructions on page 93. For the simple knife-edge pillows, refer to the basic instructions on page 18.

DESIGNER NOTE

Fabric pieces left over from large decorating projects can be combined imaginatively in pillow covers. The large box cushion on the footstool makes use of scraps from both the chair slipcover and the coverlet. It is made according to the instructions on page 93, with a zipper along the welt at one end. On the table and couch are simple knife-edge pillows, some with piping and some without, described on page 18.

Intricate cushion arm chair

This highly original design utilizes a knife-edged cushion with tabs to button it to the chair back. For the seat, a box cushion was chosen, with extending boxing strips used to tie the cushion in place. Using a variety of fabric patterns emphasizes the creative construction.

Materials

- Four coordinating printed fabrics, quantities according to chair measurements
- Pillow form or fiberfill batting for lower back cushion, 1" to 1- 1/2" (2.5 to 4 cm) thick
- Fiberfill batting for upper back cushion, 3/4" to 1" (2 to 2.5 cm) thick
- Four buttons for back cushion, approximately 1-1/2" in diameter
- Box pillow form 3-1/2" (9 cm) thick to fit chair seat, or fiberfill and muslin to make cushion liner
- Buttons for seat cushion in quantity desired, approximately 3/4" (2 cm) in diameter, and an equal number of backing buttons to use on the underside of the cushion
- Buttoning needle

Measuring and Cutting

Measure width and depth of the chair seat. Determine the thickness of the cushion if loose stuffing will be used. For the cushion top and bottom, use the width and depth measurements and add to these measurements 5/8" (1.5 cm) seam allowance on all sides.

For the boxing strips around the cushion edge, use the width and depth measurements. To each of these measurements, add approximately 12" (30 cm) at each end for the tie extensions, or the length necessary for the desired tie length. Figure the length of the decorative trim at the tie end, and subtract this length from the totals. Add seam allowances around all edges, and cut two strips for the width of the cushion and two for the depth.

For the tie facings, use the length and width of the extension part of the boxing strip/tie pieces, measuring for the trim in the same way. Add 5/8" seam allowance at the untrimmed end. Cut four pieces to these measurements.

For the back cushion, measure with the seat cushion in place from the top of the seat cushion to the desired height. Measure across the back, between the outer posts. Use separate top and bottom width measurements for this piece if the chair back is wider at the top than at the seat.

Cut the fabric for the cushion back according to measurements. For the front, cut the fabric to the width measurement, and to the length (height) desired. Add seam allowance for each piecing seam. Establish the bottom point of the upper section. For the upper cushion length, measure from this point over the top of the chair and back to the bottom point. Add 1" ease to this measurement and add seam allowances on all sides.

Cut the batting to the finished measurements of each cushion. For the tabs attaching the upper and lower sections, measure the length from a point approximately 3" to 4" (7.5 cm to 10 cm) below the top of the lower cushion section over the top of the chair to the beginning point. The tab width will depend upon the width of the chair back—the chair shown is 18" (46 cm) across and each tab is 3" wide. Add seam allowances on all sides.

Construction

1. Stitch the trim section to each boxing strip tie end and facing piece. Press the seams.

2. On facings, turn the seam allowance at the untrimmed end to wrong side; press. Stitch the facings to the tie ends with right sides together. Trim, turn right side out, and press.

3. With right sides together, pin the boxing strip/tie pieces to corresponding sides of one cushion section (the top) with the ends of the facings meeting at the corners. Stitch, ending the stitching at the corners and backstitching securely.

4. Repeat with the other cushion piece, but leave seam open across the back. Insert the pillow form and stitch across the opening.

5. On the cushion top, mark placement for the buttons. Push a buttoning needle straight through the cushion and mark the position of each corresponding backer button.

6. Sew on the buttons, sewing the decorative buttons on the cushion top to the backer buttons through the cushion. Take care to depress the cushion the same distance with each pair of buttons so the top will appear even when all buttons are in place.

7. Piece the fabrics for the front of the lower cushion as planned. Stitch the pieced front to the back with right sides together, leaving a long opening at the lower edge. Trim the corners, turn right side out, and press. Insert batting and stitch across the opening.

8. Stitch and fill the upper cushion in the same way. Stitch each tab, with fabrics right sides together, leaving an opening along one long edge for turning. Trim the corners, turn, and stitch across the opening.

9. With the cushions in place on the chair, position the tabs so the tab outer edges align with cushion outer edges. Pin. Stitch the tab to the upper cushion along the tab's long edges. Stitch the back ends of the tabs to the lower cushion. Mark button positions and sew in place, securing the tab fronts to the lower cushion.

CHAPTER 3

Designer Details

Desk chair slipcover

The back box pleat and the tie around the chair's midsection are not only decorative, but are subtle and clever devices to make the cover fit well without a lot of painstaking measuring and adjusting. Blending two complementary chintz fabrics add to the comfortable look.

Materials

- Fabrics, according to measurements
- Piping cord, 1/4" (7 mm) diameter, according to measurements

Measuring and Cutting

For a chair with curves or shaping like this one it is a good idea to make newspaper patterns for the shaped pieces using measurements taken at several different points. Allow wider seam allowances on these pieces and pin-fit them on the chair before stitching. For the chair in the photo, slight ease (approximately 1/8" or 3 mm) was added around the upper back.

Add 1/2" (1.5 cm) to measurements where seam allowance is called for. Add 1-1/2" (4 cm) at lower edges for a 3/4" (2 cm) finished double hem.

Measure the width of the seat and the depth from front to back. Add seam allowances to all sides; cut one. Mark the seamline intersections at corners.

Measure the inner back from the seat to the center point at the top back. Measure the width to the center point at the side posts. Cut a newspaper pattern and adjust the shaping, then use this pattern also to shape the upper part of the outer back. To cut from fabric, add seam allowances to all sides. Cut one.

Measure the outer back from the center point at the top back to the floor (or desired length). For a looser fit, allow the tape to hang straight from the chair back to the floor rather than closely following the line of the chair back. In this case be sure to add the same amount of ease to the width and to the back edges of the sides, extending them to the point where the back measurement was taken. Measure the width using the inner back pattern as a guide for shaping. Cut a newspaper pattern without seam/hem allowances.

Fold the pattern in half lengthwise to find the center back. Piece the newspaper to a size slightly larger than the pattern and fold it in half lengthwise. Place the folded pattern on top of the newspaper, aligning the folds. Draw around the upper back, side, and along the lower edge; remove the pattern. Flip the new pattern over. Draw a line parallel to the fold and 6-1/2" (16.5 cm) from it. This will be the inner cutting line. Add seam allowances at the upper and outer edges and hem allowance at the lower edge. Cut the pattern, and cut one left and one right from the fabric. Mark center back on the upper seamline.

For the back pleat underlay, use the back pattern and cut from folded fabric. Place the foldline of the pattern on the fabric fold, and use the inner line to cut through both thicknesses of fabric.

Measure for the skirt width around the lower point of the seat sides and front. Measure from the center point on the side posts as for the upper back sections. Extend the sides toward the back if this adjustment was made for the outer back measurement. Measure the length from the upper edge of seat. Add seam allowance on the sides and upper edge, and hem allowance at the lower edge. Cut one.

For the tie, measure around the chair back just above the seat and add approximately 2-1/2 to 3 yds (2.25 to 2.75 m) extra for bow and tie ends. The finished width is 8" (20 cm), or as desired. Cut two.

Cut bias strips to cover the piping cord, following the instructions on page 16. The length of the strips should equal the seamline measurements around the outer back and seat with extra allowed for waste at seam ends.

Construction

1. Make corded piping according to the instructions on page 16.

2. With right sides together, stitch the pleat underlay to the two back sections. Do not press the seams open. Fold the back sections together at the center back to form the box pleat. Stitch the outer back together at the center back from the upper edge to 1/2" (1.5 cm) inside the seamline, keeping the underlay free. Baste across the upper back through all thicknesses in the seam allowance.

3. Stitch piping around the seat sides and front, aligning the piping stitching line with the seat seamline.

4. Stitch the lower edge of the inner back to the back of the seat. Sew the lower front/sides to the seat, stitching on the piping stitching line.

5. Pin the sections together on the chair to check the fit. Sew the piping around the outer back section, then sew the outer back to the inner back/seat piece.

6. Stitch the tie sections with right sides together, stitching diagonally across the ends if desired. Leave an opening midway along one side for turning. Trim the corners, turn, press.

7. With the cover in place, tie the tie around the back just above the seat and arrange the bow.

Fabric and ribbon box

Are you always in search for places to stash spare change, pens, keys, and such? This clever box is both pretty to look at and a great substitute for the traditional junk drawer.

Materials

- Assorted fabrics for outer cover and lining
- Ribbon, eight pieces for corner ties
- Medium-weight cardboard
- Medium-weight fusible interfacing
- Kraft paper

Construction

1. Determine the length, width, and height of the finished box, then cut cardboard pieces for the bottom, sides, and ends.

2. Place an old sheet on the ironing board to protect the cover. (If the box will be very large, use a table for this step, covering the surface with a thick layer of newspaper to protect the top.) Carefully arrange the cardboard pieces as shown in the diagram. Leave 1/8" (3 mm) between the pieces, or slightly more space if the cardboard is more than 1/8" thick. Use a ruler or a square to check that the pieces are exactly straight and evenly spaced.

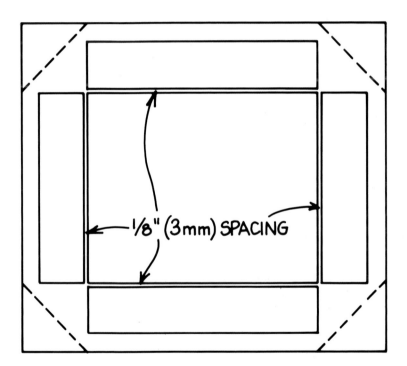

1/8" (3mm) SPACING

3. Cut a single piece of interfacing large enough to cover the cardboard pieces. Carefully lay the interfacing glue side down over the cardboard pieces. Using a dry iron (steam will warp the cardboard) and a pressing cloth, fuse the interfacing to the cardboard. It is not necessary to bond the interfacing thoroughly, it need only keep the pieces together until they are in the fabric cover.

4. Trim the interfacing close to the cardboard around the outer edges, cutting diagonally across the corners as shown by the dotted lines in the diagram.

5. Place the cardboard on a sheet of kraft paper and draw around the outer edges to make a pattern. Draw a second line 3/4" (2 cm) outside the first. This is the cutting line for the cover fabrics. Cut the box lining from the pattern. If the outer covering for the box will be a single piece of fabric, use the pattern to cut this piece too.

6. For a pieced outer cover use the pattern to arrange fabrics for piecing. Cut the pattern apart as desired to create separate pattern pieces for the patchwork. Cut fabric with these smaller pattern pieces, adding 1/4" (5 mm) at each edge where the original pattern was cut apart. Stitch the patchwork pieces together to make the outer cover, pressing each seam as it is sewn.

7. On the right side of the outer cover, position a ribbon at each end of each straight edge, 1/2" (1.5 cm) in from the corner, with the ribbon end aligned with the fabric edge. Pin or baste.

8. With right sides together, stitch the outer cover to the lining with 1/2" seam allowance, leaving one short side and the two adjacent diagonal corners open. Take care not to sew over loose ribbon ends. Trim corners and seam allowances as necessary. Turn right side out and press.

9. Insert the cardboard. Fold in the edges along the opening, press, and stitch closed by hand. Stitch around the bottom of the box, centering the stitching line in the space between the bottom and side pieces. Fold the sides up and tie ribbons to hold corners.

Fabric-decorated boxes

Simple wood boxes embellished with coordinating or complementary fabric scraps make decorative holdalls for any room in the house. The boxes also make a festive alternative to wrapping paper for special gift-giving occasions.

Materials

- Wooden boxes in assorted shapes and sizes
- Several colors of wide-top marking pens or acrylic pens
- Solid-color fabric (needed only if working with an old box that needs covering)
- Fabric scraps for embellishment
- Stiff, nonwoven fusible interfacing
- White glue
- Lightweight cardboard for templates
- Craft knife

Construction

1. If new boxes are used, color or paint the outer surface and allow to dry completely. (Refer to the Designer Note after step 5 for instructions on working with old boxes.)

2. Spread glue over the remaining surface of the lid side, the lower edge, and the inner side. Cut a fabric strip that's just a little wider and longer than the lid. Press the fabric smoothly against the glue, folding under the end where it overlaps and folding it over the edge.

3. Fuse the interfacing to the fabric scraps. Measure the perimeter of the box and divide evenly to determine the measurement for the base of the triangles and for the diagonal of the squares. Make lightweight cardboard templates for the patterns, adding a 3/8" (1 cm) hem allowance on all sides. For the wide stripes, shown on the top box, add a 3/8" (1 cm) hem allowance at each side and at the bottom. At the top the pieces should extend over the edge to the inside.

4. Cut out your fabric shapes, then cut a strip for the perimeter of the lid, adding a hem allowance as above on both sides, and an allowance for overlap at the ends. Press under the hem allowances on all pieces. (You may want to trim off the hem allowance on the templates and use them as pressing guides.) At the corners of the squares and triangles, fold the fabric straight across the corners first, then fold in at the sides. Trim away excess fabric at the corners to reduce bulk.

5. Glue the hems in place, pressing them as flat as possible. Allow to dry. Lightly mark the box with positions for decorative pieces, then glue them smoothly in place.

DESIGNER NOTE

1. From the solid color fabric, cut a circle for the lid, adding 3/4" (2 cm) to fold over the edge. The fold-over should be less than half the width of the side of the lid. Cut a strip as long as the lid's perimeter and the width of the side. Cut a second circle the size of the bottom. Cut a rectangle as wide as the perimeter of the box plus 1" (2.5 cm), and in length, the height of the box plus 2" (5 cm).

2. Spread glue evenly and thinly over the top of the lid. Let dry until slightly tacky. Place cloth wrong side up on the table and center lid on it. Smooth cloth to top of lid.

3. Working a small section at a time, spread glue along the upper half of the side. While it dries slightly, cut notches from fabric to make it lie smoothly against the edge without pleating or overlapping.

Floral showcase

If you love floral prints, these projects are for you. A small piece of needlework or just a scrap of especially pretty fabric transforms a plain cardboard box into a giftworthy accessory. The floral-print bordered napkins can be made from scratch or by rejuvenating an old napkin set.

BOTTLES WITH FLORAL DECALS

Materials

- Decorative bottle or jar
- Scrap of floral-print fabric
- Liquid fabric stiffener

Construction

1. Wash the outside of the bottle well with detergent to make sure it is free of grease and oil. Cut out a fabric motif and place it upside down on a piece of clean paper with a layer of newspapers beneath.

2. Pour a little fabric stiffener onto the fabric, enough to wet it thoroughly but not so much that it forms a puddle. Spread the stiffener carefully with a finger, taking care not to stretch the fabric or fray the edges.

3. Press the wet fabric in place on the bottle. Immediately clean any excess stiffener from around the decal with a wet cotton swab or the corner of a towel.

LIDDED BOX WITH NEEDLEWORK INSET

Materials

- Cardboard box with loose-fitting lid
- Needlework or light- to medium-weight fabric for lid inset (If you choose to work with a piece of needlework, the image area should be slightly smaller than the box lid so that a border of at least 1" (2.5 cm) can be left at the edges of the lid.)
- Lightweight cardboard, the size of the lid
- White glue
- Small, inexpensive paintbrush
- Craft knife
- Burnisher or piece of stiff cardboard
- Helpful but not essential: rotary cutter and mat

Measuring and Cutting

Determine the width of the border around the lid and cut out the central area. Measure the fabric to cover the lid. With a flexible tape measure or strip of fabric, measure over and around the edge of the lid. This will be the width of the piece. For length, measure the circumference of the outer lid and add 1".

Measure the circumference of the box and add 1". Use this measurement for the width. For length, measure the height of the box, double it, and add 1-1/2" (4 cm). Cut fabric.

Measure the width and length of the bottom of the box. Subtract 1/2" (1 cm) from each measurement, and cut two pieces of fabric this size for inside and outside of the box. Measure the length and width of the inside of the lid. Subtract 1" from each measurement and trim the lightweight cardboard to this size. Subtract 1/2" from the original measurements and cut a piece of fabric this size.

Construction

1. Position the box on the main fabric piece so that one end of the fabric extends 1/2" behind a corner of the box and one fabric edge is 3/4" (2 cm) from the bottom edge of the box. Mark box position on wrong side of fabric.

2. Spread glue thinly and evenly on the outer sides of box. Allow it to dry until slightly tacky. Place the box on the fabric in the marked position and press the fabric to the box all the way around the outer edges. At the end, turn under the fabric so that the fold is just at the corner. Add a little glue over the beginning edge of the fabric and press the folded edge in place. Use the burnisher to smooth the fabric and press the corners and edges flat.

3. Spread glue on the top edges of the box, down the inner sides, and 3/4" onto the bottom. Dry slightly, as before, then press fabric in place. Clip into the corners as necessary so the fabric will lie flat.

4. Glue the fabric around the bottom of the box on the outside, then glue the inner and outer bottom pieces in place. Glue the fabric around the lid, arranging it so the raw edges meet on the underside of the border. Work the ends as was done on the box, but place them at a different corner than those of the box so the thickness will not affect the fit of the lid.

5. Trim the needlework or fabric inset to 1/2" smaller all around than the inside of the lid. Glue it in place. Glue the light cardboard in place, centering it behind the inset. Glue the lid lining fabric over the cardboard.

NAPKINS WITH FLORAL BORDERS AND FLORAL NAPKIN RINGS

Materials

- Fabric, according to finished quantity and measurements

Construction

See page 98 for cutting and assembly instructions.

Note: The napkin rings require only some florist's wire and tape and a walk through the garden for fresh blossoms and some greenery. Just make a 2-inch (5 cm) circle from several strands of wire, wrap the wire with floral tape, and tape the stems of your blossoms and greenery in place.

Materials

- Decorator fabric, according to measurements
- Lampshade form with a wide bottom opening
- Bias tape

Measuring and Cutting

Measure the distance around the bottom ring of the form and double it. Measure the height from the top form to the bottom one and add 3" (7.5 cm) Cut out a single thickness of fabric to these measurements. Cut a strip of fabric 1-3/4" wide (4.5 cm) and as long as the upper ring's circumference plus 3/4" (2 cm).

Construction

1. Tightly wrap the upper and lower rings of the lampshade form with bias tape, then hand stitch the end points to secure.

2. Stitch the lampshade fabric together with rights sides facing with a 1/4" (6 mm) seam. Press the seam open, then press the top and bottom raw edges down 1/4" to the wrong side. Turn right side out.

3. Fold the lower edge of the fabric under the lower ring and hand stitch in place. Fold the upper edge over the upper ring. Pleat the excess fabric evenly around the ring, then hand stitch in place.

4. Press 1/4" under on the long edges of the strip and press it in half lengthwise with its right side facing out. Fold the strip over the top of the shade and hand stitch in place, turning under the overlapping raw edge when you reach the end.

SAFETY NOTE

Choose a low-wattage bulb and a wire frame that keeps the bulb a safe distance from the shade.

Fanciful footstools

These footstools illustrate three different ways to cover the same upholstered stool for three completely different effects. The top footstool is actually a simple upholstery project, while the lower two are fitted with slipcovers.

Materials

- Upholstered footstool
- Fabric, according to measurements
- Newspaper or kraft paper for pattern making
- Decorative braid in 3 colors
- White glue
- Small tacks and tack hammer
- Chalk pencil

Measuring and Cutting

For the main piece of the covering, measure the upholstered part of the stool from the lower edge of one side, across the top, to the lower edge on the other side. This will be the length of the piece.

To determine width, measure across the top to the point at which the top begins to curve downward at the side. Cut a pattern for this piece from newspaper or kraft paper.

Pin the pattern to the stool to measure for the side pieces, and make a paper pattern for these. Corners on the upper edge of the side can be left square. Add 1/2" (1.5 cm) seam allowances at the ends and upper edge of the side piece, and to the sides of the main section. Cut from fabric.

For the braid across the top, cut two strips the length of the main cover section. For the other two braids, measure the circumference of the stool at the lower edge and add 1-1/2" (4 cm) for overlap.

Construction

1. Chalk mark the seamlines on the right side of the side pieces and on the wrong side of the main section. Pin the sides to the stool, making sure the fabric's lower edges are just even with the stool's lower edge. Pin the top section in place.

2. Check that the seamlines match, and use the main section seamline as a guide to round the corners of the side pieces. Mark the new seamlines on the sides with chalk.

3. Carefully remove the pieces, then use a round household object to even up the corner seamlines on the side pieces. Cut off the excess fabric around the corners, leaving 1/2" seam allowance.

4. Stitch the sides to the main section with right sides together. Press the seams toward the main section. Place the cover on the stool and pin the strips of braid to the main section approximately 1/2" inside seamlines.

5. Stitch the braid by machine with a zigzag stitch set at medium width and length. If the braid is particularly heavy it may be easier to sew with the embroidery foot or appliqué foot.

6. Return the cover to the stool. Beginning at one corner, glue two remaining braid strips in place. Apply glue evenly to the cover, a small section at a time, and let dry until tacky. Press a section of braid in place, stretching it slightly and pressing firmly. Tack invisibly at intervals. Turn under and glue the end of the strip and allow it to dry before gluing it to the cover.

Materials

- Fabric, according to measurements
- Thick decorative cording with tasseled end, or corded drapery tiebacks with tassels
- Optional: a large decorative or fabric-covered button

Measuring and Cutting

Measure the length and width of the stool top. For the sides, measure from the top to approximately 1" (2.5 cm) below the lower edge of the upholstered section of the stool, or to desired length.

Make a paper pattern for the top. Find a round object of the appropriate size and round the corners slightly. Mark the corner point on each seamline. Add 1/2" (1.5 cm) seam allowance on all sides.

The cutting width of the side pieces will depend upon the fabric's width. If the fabric width allows, cut the sides as one continuous piece to the side measurements total (before seam allowances were added) of top piece. Add

seam allowance at each end. If this section must be pieced, be sure to place the seams at the corners. Add 1/2" at upper edge(s) and 1-1/2" (4 cm) at lower edge(s). Mark the corner points on the upper edge seamline.

Construction

1. Stitch the ends of the side pieces, right sides together, to form a ring. Stitch the sides to the top, matching the marked corners.

2. Place the cover over the stool to check hemline. For the hem, press the lower edge 1-1/2" to wrong side. Turn under raw edge 1/2" and press again. Stitch close to the inner fold.

3. With the cover in place, arrange the cords and tassels. If drapery tiebacks are used, knot them together at the center of the stool and stitch in place by hand. Tasseled cords may be cut to the desired length and tacked in place, with the cut ends meeting at the center of the cover top. Sew a large button to the cover to hide the ends.

Materials

- Upholstered footstool
- Fabric, two solid colors for cover and complementary pattern for piping, according to measurements
- Piping cord, 1/4" to 3/8" (.5 to 1 cm) diameter, according to measurements
- Newspaper or kraft paper for pattern making

Measuring and Cutting

Measure the stool as described in the instructions for the tasseled footstool. Cut a paper pattern to the finished measurements for the top. Cut another for one or two sides, depending on whether the stool is rectangular or square.

Fold the top pattern in half and mark a cutting line for the centered inset stripe. Fold one side pattern and mark in the same way. Make a pattern for each new top section, adding 1/2" (1.5 cm) seam allowance where each cut was made and at the outer edges. Cut two for the outer sections from the main color and one center inset from the accent color.

Mark one of the side patterns in the same way, planning the inset stripe to match with that on the top. At each side of the piece also add 2" (5 cm) for the pleat. Add seam allowance to the top of the pieces, and at the lower edge add 2" hem allowance. Cut four end sections from the main color, and two of the center section from the accent color.

RED AND WHITE COVER WITH STRIPED PIPING

For the plain side piece, add seam, hem, and pleat allowances as above. Cut two.

For the pleat underlay, cut four pieces each 5" (13 cm) wide. For cutting length add 1/2" seam allowance at the upper edge and 2" hem allowance at the lower edge.

Cut bias strips to cover piping, following instructions on page 16.

Construction

1. Piece the top, sewing the centered stripe to the edge sections with right sides together. Mark corner points on the seamline. Sew the piping to the right side of the top according to the instructions on page 24.

2. Piece the two sides with the insets. Stitch the ends of the pleat underlays to the ends of the side pieces with right sides together. Do not press these seams open.

3. On each side piece, at the upper seamline, mark a point 2" from the underlay seamline. Bring the marked points together to create the box pleat at each corner. On the wrong side, stitch each pleat down approximately 2" from the upper edge.

4. With right sides together, stitch the top to the sides, matching the corners and aligning the inset stripes. Hem the lower edge with a hand or machine blind hem.

Patchwork vase

Create a custom patchwork vase in less than an hour with these simple, no-sew techniques. Feel free to use several coordinating print fabrics or to mix and match prints with solid fabrics.

Materials

- 2 large pieces of tracing paper
- Narrow tape (1/4" to 3/8"), (6 mm to 9 mm)
- Coordinating fabric scraps
- Fabric stiffener or fabric glue

Construction

1. Wrap the tissue paper loosely around the vase to get a rough idea of the size of the surface area. Stretch the tape across the tissue paper at varying angles to break up the space in interesting shapes.

2. Trace the outside edges of all the tape, then gently peel the tape off. Place the second piece of tissue paper on top of the first and trace the patterns. Set it aside to use as a position reference.

3. Cut out all of the tissue paper shapes to create patterns, then cut out the fabric. Soak the fabric shapes in fabric stiffener and press them in place against the vase, referring to the second piece of tissue paper for position references and leaving blank space in the areas once taken up by the tape.

4. Press out any wrinkles in the fabric and blot up the excess stiffener.

Materials

- A variety of fabric scraps
- Optional time-saver: rotary cutter and mat

Measuring and Cutting

The finished size of the bags in the photograph is 4" x 6" (12 cm x 16 cm). The seam allowance, included in all cutting dimensions, is 1/4" (.5 cm).

For each bag, cut 18 2" (5 cm) fabric squares. For the top band, cut one piece 9-1/2" x 2-1/4" (25 cm x 6 cm). For the tie, cut one piece, on the bias if desired, 2" x 10-1/2" (5 cm x 16 cm).

Sachet bags are quick and easy to make from your favorite fabric scraps. Make several at a time and keep them on hand for gift-giving emergencies. Fill the sachets with dried herbs from the garden or a purchased potpourri, or raid the pantry for cinnamon sticks and cloves.

Construction

1. Stitch the squares with right sides together to make six vertical rows of three squares each. Stitch the rows together to form a rectangle.

2. With right sides together stitch band to upper edge of patchwork, double-checking to press each seam before stitching across it.

3. Stitch together along the end and lower edge. Turn under the raw edge 1/2" (1.5 cm) along the top; press. Turn the edge under to the foldline; press and stitch.

4. Fold the tie in half lengthwise with right sides together. Stitch across the ends, on the diagonal if preferred, and along the long edge, leaving an opening of 1-1/2" (4 cm) midway for turning. Trim the corners, turn, press, and stitch across the opening.

Fabric frames

Cut from a single piece of fabric with no mitered corners, these mats are quick to make. Assemble them in groups and play with different colors and prints for the bows.

Materials

- Picture frames
- Purchased mats
- Assorted fabrics, according to measurements
- White glue
- Small tacks or staple gun

Measuring and Cutting

Cut a fabric rectangle approximately 1" (2.5 cm) larger all around than the mat, taking care to cut with the fabric grainline or pattern.

For the main part of each bow, cut a strip to the desired finished length plus 1/2" (1 cm) seam allowances, and twice the desired width plus 1/2" seam allowances. A smaller strip forms the knot around the bow and attaches to the frame to hang the picture. The finished size of this piece is slightly narrower than the main part of the bow and can be made any desired length. Add seam allowances as for the main bow.

Construction

1. Form the main part of the bow. Fold the fabric strip in half lengthwise with right sides together. Mark a diagonal line across each end as a guide for stitching. Stitch one end, using a very short stitch length at the beginning and around the corner. Stitch nearly to the center of the long edge, then leave an opening for turning. Stitch the remaining long edge and end. Turn, press, and stitch across the opening.

2. Make the narrow bow strip as above, but stitch the ends straight across rather than on the diagonal. Place the fabric for the mat wrong side up on a table. Position the mat and lightly mark corner positions on the fabric. Spread glue thinly and evenly over the front surface of the mat and let it dry until slightly tacky. Press the mat onto the fabric and smooth the fabric over the front, taking care not to stretch it.

3. Cut away the center of the fabric, leaving approximately 1" around the inner edge. Carefully clip from the center to within about 1/8" (3 mm) of the cardboard at each inner corner. Spread glue along the inner edge and over to the back. Glue fabric as above. Work around the outer edge in the same way.

Potpourri bags

Have you ever assembled one of those quick scrap projects and found yourself disappointed with the results? Choosing special fabrics and trims — instead of just any old scrap fabric from the back of the closet — makes for great results every time. This project is quick to assemble and makes a special gift or a fragrant pick-me-up for any room in the home.

- Two small pieces of complementary fabric
- Decorative cord, 1-1/4 yds (1.2 m)
- Embroidery floss or silk thread to wrap cord ends
- White glue
- Fragrant dried blooms or commercially prepared potpourri

Construction

1. Cut two 13" x 9" (33 cm x 23 cm) rectangles, one for the outer bag and one for the lining. With the right sides together, stitch the two pieces along one long edge. Fold the fabric in half, right sides together, and stitch one long edge and across the end of the outer bag.

2. Turn right side out so that the raw edges of the lining fabric extend beyond sewn end of the outer bag. Turn in seam allowances in the lining, press, and stitch close to the folds through all thicknesses. Turn the lining to the inside.

3. To prevent the cord ends from fraying, wrap them tightly with tape approximately 1" (2.5 cm) from the ends. Cover the tape with multiple wraps of embroidery floss, silk buttonhole thread, or any other decorative thread that strikes your fancy. Tuck the ends under and seal with a dot of white glue.

Fabric book cover

This festive book cover is made from linen scraps with patchwork insets on the front and back. Make one for all your favorite books — the guest book, address book, even the TV Guide. The covers of the book slip into flaps, and the book is tied closed with colorful ribbon.

Materials

- Solid color linen for outer cover
- Contrast fabric for lining and inner flaps
- Scraps of four coordinating print fabrics for patchwork insets on front and back
- Ribbon for tie
- Fusible interfacing for outer cover
- Book to be covered

Measuring and Cutting

For the outer cover and lining, with the book closed, measure the width from the outer edge of the front cover, around the spine, and to the outer edge of the back cover. Measure the height. For ease, add to each edge 1/4" (1 cm) for thinner fabric and 1/2" (2.5 cm) for thicker fabric. Add 1/2" (1.5 cm) seam allowances on all edges. From these measurements, cut one piece from outer fabric, one piece from lining fabric, and one piece of interfacing.

For the flaps, the finished width should be slightly less than half the width of the book's cover. Add to this measurement 1-1/2" (4 cm) for hem and seam allowance. For height, use the measurement for the outer cover. Cut two pieces of outer fabric to these measurements.

For the patchwork, first determine the size of the finished patchwork insets to allow a border around the edges and to extend to the edge of the spine. Figure the finished size of the individual patchwork squares, then add 1/4" to each edge for seam allowances. Cut the number of pieces needed.

Note: It's easier to cut multiple pieces for patchwork with a rotary cutter and mat, using a heavy ruler to guide the cutter. As an alternative, make a cardboard template to use as a cutting guide to make sure all pieces are identical.

Construction

1. Fuse the interfacing to the wrong side of the outer cover. Stitch the patchwork pieces together, using a 1/4" seam allowance. Stitch the pieces to create horizontal rows, press seams, then stitch rows together. Press under 1/4" around the outer edge of the finished patchwork. With thicker fabrics, it may be easier to first stitch 1/4" all around the edge, then fold and press on the stitching line.

2. Position the patchwork pieces on the outer cover section. Stitch in place with a zigzag stitch and contrasting thread. Hem one long edge of each flap section with a 1" (2.5 cm) double hem. Position one flap section at each end of the lining piece, with wrong sides of flaps against right side of lining and raw edges aligned. Pin or baste.

3. Pin the lining to the outer piece, with right sides together. Stitch, leaving an opening of 2" to 3" (5 cm to 8 cm) at the lower back for turning. At the corners, take a very small stitch or two on the diagonal so the corners will turn neatly. Trim seam allowances as necessary, turn right side out, and press. Stitch across the opening. Center the ribbon on the spine; stitch through all thicknesses.

Fabric-covered picture mats

This project makes a quick, inexpensive way to create custom picture frames. Use them to frame a favorite New Yorker cartoon, an invitation to a memorable party, or a child's art-work.

Materials

- Stiff, noncorrugated cardboard or foamcore mat board, or purchased mat
- Mat knife or craft knife
- Carpenter's square
- Assorted fabrics
- White glue
- Burnisher

Construction

1. Cut the cardboard mat to the desired size using the carpenter's square and knife. Cut four strips of fabric, one for each side of the mat. Each should be the length of the side plus 1" (3 cm), and wide enough to reach completely around each side of the mat and meet on the back. Position the fabric so that patterns will match at mitered corners.

2. On the front surface of the mat measure between the inner corners and between the outer corners, and the diagonal from the inner to the outer corner. Mark these points on the wrong side of each strip.

3. Place two strips with their right sides together and their corner markings aligned. Stitch the diagonal seam to miter the corners, beginning and ending the seam exactly at the marked inner and outer corner points. Do not backstitch the seams, but leave long thread tails for minor adjustments later. Trim the seam allowances to 1/2" (1.5 cm) and press open. Do not press the unstitched area at the corners.

4. Place the fabric wrong side up on a table and position the mat on it to check that the corners align. Spread glue evenly and thinly on the front surface of the mat, working one side at a time. Allow the glue to dry until tacky. Press the fabric in place, working the corners first, then the center, then the area between, taking care not to distort the fabric. Glue the outer edges next, then the inner edges. Last, glue the back, clipping the fabric as necessary to neaten the corners.

Room divider

Decorative cutwork patterns allow light to pass through this fabric screen. The screen's pockets provide clever, always-welcome storage space. Screens made for fabric inserts can be purchased at building supply and unfinished furniture stores.

- Purchased folding screen
- Fabric, according to measurements
- Firm, lightweight fusible interfacing for main fabric pieces
- Trim for pockets (double-fold bias tape or any firm ribbon)
- For optional cutwork: fusible bonding web, washable fabric marker

Measuring and Cutting

For the width of the panels, measure between the frame uprights. Add 1-1/2" (4 cm) at each side for hems. Measure for length from the top center of the upper rod to the bottom center of the lower rod. Add a total of 1" (2.5 cm) for seam allowances. From these measurements cut a front and a back panel and two pieces of fusible interfacing for each divider section.

Cut two pockets for each divider section, one from each fabric. The pocket is the same width as the main panel. Finished length is according to preference; on the screen in the photo the pocket is slightly less than 1/3 the panel length. To the finished length measurement add 1" at the upper edge for a double hem and 1/2" (1.5 cm) seam allowance at the bottom.

Ribbon or trim pieces should be long enough at each side of the panel to extend around the frame. Cut three for the front and three for the back.

Construction

1. Fuse interfacing to the wrong side of each panel. Double-hem the upper edge of each pocket section.

2. Position the pocket section on the panel with the pocket's wrong side facing the panel's right side, and with the lower edge and sides aligned. Machine baste around the three sides in the seam/hem allowance.

3. Hem the sides of the panels. Turn under 1-1/2" to the wrong side; press. Turn under raw edge 1/2"; press. Stitch close to the inner fold.

4. Center the trim along the pocket's upper edge. Stitch the trim to the pocket along both edges, beginning and ending as close as possible to the side hems. Stitch through all thicknesses between the end of the first stitching lines and panel edges.

5. Stitch vertical lines through the pocket and the panel to create smaller individual pockets as desired. Stitch the panels with right sides together across the upper and lower ends. Turn and press. With the double panel right side out, stitch across the upper and lower edges to create casings.

6. Work a cutwork design, if desired. Position the panel with edges aligned, then draw designs on the fabric with a washable marker. Fuse the bonding web behind the marked design areas between the panel layers. Cut away the design areas.

7. Set the machine for a zigzag stitch with medium width and short length. Overcast the edges of the design areas. Place the fabric panels in the divider sections. Pull the pocket trim extensions taut around the frame and tack or staple in place.

Fabric wainscot

An innovative way to transform a room, this design is easy to change with the seasons. Strips of wooden coat pegs, the sort available for hallways and children's rooms, support a panel of stiffened fabric. Fabrics manufactured specifically for home decorating are especially good for this project because they are treated with finishing agents for added stability and stain resistance.

Materials

- Coat-peg strips (a length of 1x2 and drawer pulls can be substituted)
- Fabrics for the main panel, borders, facings, and tabs, according to measurements
- Firm fusible interfacing

Measuring and Cutting

Install the peg strips before you begin measuring to ensure accuracy. To accommodate slight stretching of fabric, allow 1/2" to 1" (1.5 cm to 2.5 cm) between the lower edge of the panel and the floor. Determine the placement of the upper edge of the panel. Determine the finished width of the border and the finished width of the central panel. For the tab length measure from the lower edge of the upper border, over the peg, and back to starting point.

For the central panel, add 1/2" seam allowance to each edge. For borders, cut strips to desired width, adding seam allowances on both edges. Cut border pieces to the finished length of the complete panel plus seam allowances at both ends. Cut facing pieces the same size as borders. Cut interfacing for the central panel and four border sections. For tabs, cut strips 2-1/2" (6 cm) wide and to finished length measurement plus 1" (3 cm) seam allowances.

Construction

1. Fuse the interfacing to the wrong side of the central panel and border sections according to manufacturer's instructions.

2. With right sides together, stitch the border pieces to the outer edges of central panel. Miter the corners as described on page 19. Trim corner seams. Press seam allowances toward the border.

3. Make the tabs. With right sides together stitch the long edges with a 1/4" (.5 cm) seam. Turn right sides out, press, and edgestitch both long edges.

4. Overlap the ends of the tabs, aligning the raw edges, and pin along the top border with the loop toward the center panel and the unfinished ends extending beyond the seamline the same width as the border measurements. Baste.

5. With right sides together, stitch the border facing to the border around the outer edges. Miter the corners as for the border. Press the inner edge of the facing to the inside so that it just covers the facing's stitching line. On the right side, stitch through all layers along the facing/central panel seamline. Trim off the tab ends. Stitch across the tabs close to outer border edge.

Floral play

These floral fabric boxes are of the same classic design used by rare-book collectors to store unbound signatures or keep fragile old volumes intact. The traditional fabric for these boxes is "buckram," a heavily starched, even-weave cotton fabric available from bookbinding suppliers. Coordinating chairs and a simple piped pillow complete the room's look.

Materials

- 1/2 yard (.5 m) tightly woven cotton or linen fabric, of medium to heavy weight and very stable

- Fusible interfacing (needed only if your chosen fabric needs stiffening)

- Lining, approximately 18" x 8" (46 cm x 20 cm), (traditionally marbled paper, but silk scraps or a fancy gift wrap can be substituted)

- Sturdy, noncorrugated cardboard 1/8" (3 mm) thick, approximately 26" x 12" (66 cm x 31 cm)

- Ribbon for ties, 32" (82 cm)

- White glue

- Sharp, heavy-duty craft knife

- Burnishing tool, such as bookbinder's bone folder

- Paste brush

- Small metal carpenter's square

Measuring and Cutting

Cut out the cardboard with the square and a sharp knife. Cut two pieces, 8" x 12 " (20.5 cm x 30.5 cm) for the outer covers. For the spine cut one, 2-1/4" x 12" (5.8 cm x 30.5 cm). Cut three pieces for sides of the base: two at 2-1/4" x 7-1/2" (5.8 cm x 19.3 cm) and one at 2-1/4" x 11" (5.8 cm x 28.1 cm). For sides of the lid cut three pieces: two at 2-1/4" x 7-3/4" (5.8 cm x 19.9 cm) and one at 2-1/4" x 11-1/2" (5.8 cm x 29.3 cm).

Cut out the fabric. For the outer cover, cut one piece 21" x 10-1/2" (53 cm x 26.5 cm). For the spine, cut one piece 11-1/2" x 3-3/4" (29.3 cm x 9.5 cm). For the edges cut two pieces, 29" x 6" (74 cm x 15 cm). For the lining, cut out one piece, 17-3/4" x 7 1/4" (45 cm x 18.5 cm).

Construction

1. If necessary, fuse backing to all fabric pieces (except lining) according to manufacturer's instructions. Place the outer fabric wrong side up on a table. Arrange the outer cover cardboard pieces on the fabric, with the spine piece between. Leave 1/8" (3 mm) between the edges of the spine and the outer cover pieces. Align the upper and lower edges of the three pieces, and have equal margins of fabric around the outer edges. Outline the pieces with pencil. Remove the cardboard. Draw diagonal lines across the outer corners, 1/8" outside each marked corner. Cut away the fabric along the diagonal lines.

2. Spread glue evenly over the cloth. Press the cardboard in place. When slightly dry, turn over and smooth with the burnisher. Using the burnisher, fold the fabric up at the corners along the diagonal cut. Fold over one edge of the cloth, rubbing along the edge with the burnisher. Apply a little glue on the cloth where the next side will overlap at the corner, then fold over the next edge. If the glue dries too quickly, add more glue sparingly. Continue around all edges. Use the burnisher to define the crease between the covers and the spine.

3. Position the fabric for the spine, centering it top to bottom on the inside. Mark the position with a pencil as for the outer covers, and glue the area. Smooth the fabric in place and define the creases with the burnisher.

4. Glue the ties in place. Position one at the center of each outer edge, the end approximately 1" (2.5 cm) in from the cover edge. Glue 3/4" (2 cm) of the end; press flat.

5. To make the base of the box, spread glue on the edges of both ends of the longer cardboard strip. Stand the strips on their long edges and press the two shorter pieces to the glued ends of the longer piece to form right angles, using the carpenter's square as a guide to make sure the corners are exactly square. Allow to dry.

6. Spread glue on the outer side and edges of cardboard. Working on the outside first, glue to the fabric strip, positioning one edge of the cardboard 1" from one edge of the fabric. Stand the cardboard on the edge at the short side of the fabric with the short fabric extensions inside the cardboard U. Clip the fabric in toward the corners of the cardboard so the fabric will press flat. Keep checking that the corners remain square.

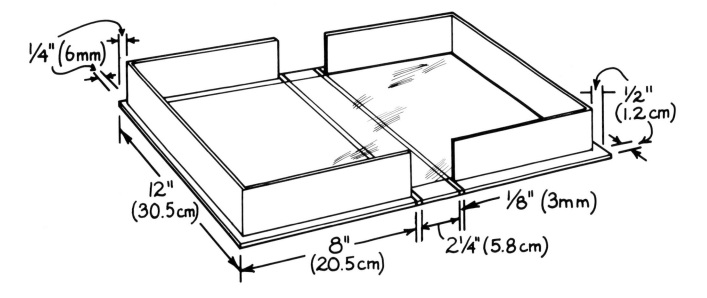

1/4" (6mm)

12"
(30.5 cm)

8"
(20.5 cm)

2 1/4" (5.8 cm)

1/8" (3mm)

1/2"
(1.2 cm)

7. Trim the remaining fabric to lie flat at the inside of the base. Clip at the inner corners, cutting the fabric just to the inside of the cardboard's edge. Fold the fabric ends around to the inside. Cut away a square so that the fabric folds smoothly over upper edge to inside. Spread glue on cardboard and glue remaining fabric in place with piece on edge. Clip into the corners of the fabric extensions at the bottom so they will press flat with the base standing on edge.

8. Position the base on the cover with the ends at the open side even with the inner edge of one side of the cover and the other three sides 1/2" (1.2 cm) from the cover's outer edges. Lightly mark the position on the cover. Spread a line of glue 3/4" wide inside the marks. Press the base in place, using the burnisher to smooth out the fabric extensions.

9. Construct the lid as you did the base. Glue it to the cover, making sure to position it with 1/4" (7 mm) around the outer edges and so that the open edge aligns with the cover edge at the spine. Turn the fabric extensions under at the ends of the piece so they are even with edges of lid and glue smoothly in place.

10. Open the box flat and measure for the lining. Trim the lining to exactly the inner base length measurement. For width, measure across the inside of the box from outer edge of base to outer edge of lid, and add 1/4". Spread glue and press the lining in place, pressing well into the spine creases.

PILLOW AND DIRECTOR'S CHAIRS

Construction

1. For the corded, knife-edge pillow, refer to the basic materials, cutting, and assembly instructions on page 18.

2. For the chairs, refer to the fabric criteria and construction steps described on page 99.

Index